In this beautifully written book Simon Ponsonby invites us to stand back and take in who Jesus is. The result is profound. I encourage everyone to pick this book up and read it – and I strongly suspect that you too will conclude that Jesus is amazing!

DR. AMY ORR-EWING
Director, OCCA The Oxford Centre for Christian Apologetics

Simon Ponsonby is more than a good writer – he is a passionate follower of Jesus whose love for his Lord shines out in his life as well as in the pages he pens. *Amazed by Jesus* is approachable but deep, reminding us that at the centre of everything is Jesus. Read it and discover, or rediscover, just how amazing Jesus is.

MARK SAYERS
Senior Leader Red Church Melbourne, Australia;
Author of *Strange Days* and *Reappearing Church*

In the pulpit of the church I attended as a student, Charles Simeon, a great preacher of the late 18th and early 19th century, had the words from John 12:21 carved, visible only to the preacher, 'Sir, we would see Jesus'. This is a great reminder of the preacher's task and of the greatest need of each human heart – and why I am so grateful to Simon for this wonderful book. Read and reflect and see Jesus afresh!

PAUL HARCOURT
National Leader of New Wine

This is a book born in amazement and contemplation. And it is a book that can stir that same amazement. It is my conviction that fascination for the person of Jesus Christ is the most urgent need for the church in the west. We have to rediscover the source of it all. This book filled with poetic, colourful descriptions is a real help to deepen the core of our faith: the relationship with Jesus.

DR JOHANNES HARTL
Founder of the Augsburg House of Prayer;
Author of *Heart Fire*, *Simply Pray* and *God Untamed*

CW00552040

Whilst deeply theological, this is not primarily a theology book. While profoundly insightful, this is not a new revelation, while richly Christocentric, this is not a book simply about Christ. It is in fact a trap door into a world of treasure that leaves you breathless with wonder and more intoxicated than ever with the God-man Jesus. Read it devotionally and fall in love all over again. I did!

DR NIC HARDING

Director, Kairos Connexion; Director, Together for the Harvest;

Founding Pastor, Frontline Church

After years of books on church growth strategies, prayer, revival, the gifts of the Holy Spirit, the seven steps to who knows what, and countless more subjects, here in *Amazed by Jesus* Simon Ponsonby draws us back to our first love, to Jesus himself, the lover of our souls.

The author takes us gently by the hand and leads us to Jesus. He brings us carefully, respectfully into his presence, so that sometimes we feel almost as if we are personally present as he turns water to wine, or speaks to a pharisee, or heals a leper, or teaches his disciples. Ponsonby opens our eyes afresh to the wonder of the man, Christ Jesus.

It is very quickly obvious that the book is written from a lifetime of meditation on the person and character of Jesus, of spending time in his presence, of being taken up in awe of him. We are fortunate indeed to be drawn into this special relationship.

Revelation 2 contains the serious warning to the church at Ephesus that in spite of all their hard work, their perseverance, their godly discernment, and more, they had forsaken their first love. The call is to repent. In this lovely book, Simon Ponsonby takes us to Jesus, encouraging us to spend time in his presence, to gaze on his beauty, to fall in love with him again. And yes, to repent of our busy-ness in this current age, and to return to our first love.

DR GARTH GILMOUR

This is a sparkling book that is beautifully written and arresting. Full to the brim with learning and wisdom, it overflows with love for Jesus. An unforgettable and virtuoso work that both feeds the mind and warms the heart.

J JOHN

Minister, Speaker and Author

I would find it incredibly difficult to overstate the impact Simon Ponsonby has had on my life to date. He has been a mentor and friend, an encourager and guide, and along the journey his writings and teachings have been a stream in the desert. From the words that come out of his mouth when he preaches, to the prose he puts on paper, Simon's ability to blend scripturally sound exegesis, with the revelation and experience he has himself received from his own relationship with Christ, give him the rare ability to quench people's spiritual thirst, and facilitate a greater hunger to know and receive the 'more' Jesus has for each of us. At a time when the world advocates many precepts and propositions as the means to advancement, Simon's book re-orientates our hearts and minds back to the person and work of Jesus. I believe this book is not only an encouraging voice for the church at this time, but is also a necessary vessel that will impart a renewed delight in Jesus, deposit a fresh revelation of timeless Biblical truths, and inspire us to intentionally desire a deeper devotion to Jesus our Lord in every area of our lives.

REV ROB WALL

Writer; Teacher; TBN Programmer and Presenter

Out of the many theological books published, there are few dynamic, succinct and faithful expositions of the central character of the Christian story – Jesus Christ himself. Simon Ponsonby's *Amazed by Jesus* is one such book. In Simon's engaging and inimitable style, he weaves story, quotations and testimony together with incisive Biblical exegesis. This is practical theology at its best, pointing the reader to the Biblical Christ and the only logical and reasonable response is worship.

GREG DOWNES

Director of Ministerial Training, Wycliffe Hall, Oxford University

Gordon and I had the privilege to work on team with Simon Ponsonby at St Aldates Church in Oxford for nearly 7 years. During this time, I learnt to admire Simon's ability to mix complex theological truth with his wonderful sense of humour and storytelling. *Amazed by Jesus* illustrates that he is still a powerful communicator. This book will agitate and capture your heart for this amazing Jesus once again. As you read this book you need to eat it slowly, chewing the depths of the truths, lingering and partaking deeply of this Jesus without being in a hurry. Then I believe you will be able to take the challenge and live a Jesus life, knowing that the best is still to come!

RACHEL HICKSON

Founder of Heartcry for Change; International Author and Speaker

If there's one thing I've learned about Simon Ponsonby through a decade of ministering together in Oxford, it's that he loves to speak about Jesus. Many of these chapters I've heard Simon preach, chatted about over coffee, or discussed in text message exchanges and each one is a love song to the Lord. All together, the effect is like Handel's 'Messiah': a beautiful and rich expression of the person and work of Christ from all angles. Read, listen, and be amazed again by Messiah who is its great theme.

DANIEL HAMES

Associate Director, Union School of Theology

Simon Ponsonby has developed a signature ability to take deep theological truths and make them accessible to everyone. He writes with the thoroughness of a scholar and the heart of a pastor. The richness of his work reflects a profound grasp of history, art, and literature woven together in a rich tapestry of compelling prose. In *Amazed by Jesus*, Simon powerfully tells the story of Jesus for the 21st century reader – who reading this will want to love Jesus.

REV DR BARRY CRANE

Senior Pastor North Sound Church and United States Navy Chaplain (Ret.)

Most Christian leaders and speakers have one key life message that ends up being woven into all they do and say. Simon's is here, loud and clear: Jesus is amazing! Come to him. He shines a spotlight on his magnificent hero, his Lord and his King and illuminates the power, the beauty, the wonder of who Jesus Christ really is. It's almost impossible to read this book and not be captured and captivated by the wonder of Jesus and then in turn want to give the whole of your life over to Him (again!). Each chapter is rich with stories that inspire and challenge and I found my heart being warmed, my spirit energised and my resolve sharpened to live in such a way that glorifies Jesus, who is, quite simply, amazing.

NESS WILSON

Leader of Pioneer UK and Open Heaven Church Loughborough

A feast of beautiful prose which explains deep truths of Jesus in a simple way. Whether you are walking in the valley or on the mountaintop in your life, Jesus is brought near in the pages of this book. Every ounce of wisdom and knowledge that Simon possesses of Jesus is wrung out here and communicated from a heart that loves Jesus and earnestly desires that we know what he knows of Jesus. A treasure of a book.

BARONNESS ELIZABETH BERRIDGE

What a beautifully written book my dear friend Simon has composed. I realized in reading *Jesus is Amazing* that oftentimes the focus in Church tends to be on the Father and the Holy Spirit, both of which are needed, yet also where perhaps we have overlooked the person of Jesus. With the historical content, this book truly reflects and speaks of depths of the person of Jesus layered with personal connections to draw us into closer and deeper relationship to the One who sees us. It's a beautiful reminder to know that we are truly seen, loved and accepted and how this reminder changes everything. We are loved to love and our hope is found in this love, to be loved by Jesus now and to be with Him forever. Simon does a tremendous job of reminding us; at times teaching us, all the while pointing to what a magnificent and very personal gift Jesus is to us. Simon has such a gift of taking deep theological truths and making them attainable for all. This book does not disappoint and I have no doubt those who will engage in this journey will only fall more in love with our amazing Jesus.

CHRISTY WIMBER
Author and pastor. ChristyWimber.com

When I think of Simon, I think of colour, vibrancy, humour, kindness, encouragement, friendship and grace (among many other things) This book is bursting at the seams with all of these. But above all I think of his lifelong love of Jesus Christ; his uncompromising devotion to Jesus Christ, and his relentless commitment to introducing Jesus Christ to whoever he can, whenever he can. In this book, Simon has drawn back the myriad veils that obscure the face and person of Jesus in our wayward culture, and beats a path to his spectacular presence. This book offers a true theophany to anyone with an open heart. Read it and your life will be transformed as you encounter the glory of God in Christ.

ANITA CLEVERLY
Church Leader; Author; Teacher

If you want to be acquainted with the person of Jesus – or, as Einstein put it, to be 'enthralled by the luminous figure of the Nazarene' – look no further than this book. Writing in a radically personal way, and drawing upon a wealth of allusion, Simon Ponsonby paints a highly attractive and deeply compelling picture of the founder of the Christian faith.

JAMES MUMFORD
Ethicist and Author of *Vexed: Ethics Beyond Political Tribes* (Bloomsbury, 2020)

# AMAZED

*by*

# JESUS

# AMAZED
*by*
# JESUS

## SIMON PONSONBY

FOREWORD BY RICO TICE

**Muddy**
Pearl

Published in 2020 by
Muddy Pearl, Edinburgh, Scotland.
www.muddypearl.com
books@muddypearl.com

Reprinted 2023

*British Library Cataloguing in Publication Data*

A catalogue record for this book is available from the British Library

HB ISBN 978-1-910012-97-0
PB ISBN 978-1-910012-96-3

Typeset in Minion by Revo Creative Ltd, Lancaster

Printed in Great Britain by Bell & Bain Ltd, Glasgow

*For my mum*

# FOREWORD

All Souls, Langham Place, the church where I work, is familiar to many from the BBC News opening sequence, where multi-coloured lasers are seen flashing over the spire. If you visit us at the top of Regent Street, as many do, when you walk into the main church your eye will immediately be drawn to the painting above the communion table at the front. It was a gift to the church from George IV in 1825 and is called *Ecce Homo*, which is Latin for 'Behold the man'. It is, of course, a depiction of Christ from John 19:5: 'When Jesus came out wearing the crown of thorns and the purple robe, Pilate said to them, "Here is the man!"' On countless occasions over the last twenty-seven years whilst on staff I have counted it a great privilege to explain to visitors that of course this is Jesus, the Lamb of God, laying down his life, and enduring mockery, whilst being forced to wear the twisted perversions of royal regalia – a purple robe and a crown of thorns.

Now hold on to your seats, for this book has made an indelible mark on me – it has made me ponder for the first time in twenty-seven years what Jesus would see. So, Simon muses, 'What if Pilate has said this in the vocative, addressing Jesus, "Man, look", what would Jesus see?' I confess, that when it comes to this painting, I'd only ever thought about what *I* see, looking at Jesus. I'd never asked what *he* sees, looking at me. So, this morning I found myself walking up to that picture in All Souls and gazing at it with fresh eyes, as though for the first time. The focus is of course the central figure of Christ and despite the grotesque and even caricatured individuals abusing him, as I studied the picture today Jesus seems to see the New Creation with a look of resigned long suffering, but also a forgiving confidence. And it's as though he's demanding a response from us as if to say:

'Whose side are you on?'

So, thank you, Simon, after twenty-seven years you've totally refreshed my tour of All Souls and you've focused it much more profoundly on helping people to be amazed at Jesus.

But it doesn't stop there, I also discovered in this book that there are numerous other depictions of this scene from John 19:5. There's Titian, Caravaggio and Matsys, to name but a few. And now I can see the opportunity for evangelism. What is the face of Jesus doing in each picture? Let's look together. And how does that help us understand Christ's mission to go to the cross?

Having read the book this morning and visited the picture this afternoon, I'm now online researching a talk to help us reflect on what Jesus is suffering and thinking as he goes to the cross, and we've got art and church history to help us.

To my delight Simon is still not done. He's got an extraordinary contemporary story too of an 80-year-old amateur artist in Borja, Spain, who took it upon herself to restore Martinez's 'Ecce Homo' in 2012, and brought 200,000 visitors to the town in the process, which was a huge boost to a declining local economy.

So that's a little cameo of what this remarkable book about Jesus has done for me. Honestly, my heart is beating with the thrill of it and I can only hope you will have a similar experience, as Simon calls each of us afresh to be amazed by Jesus, and then, as Minister of Theology for over twenty-five years at St Aldates, Oxford, he also brings so much from Scripture, history, contemporary culture, family life and pastoral care to help us see Jesus afresh.

This is so needed too, and I for one could certainly relate to the stark question which Simon had the courage to face in the first three paragraphs of this book:

'Do I love Jesus, or do I just work for him?'

As our Lord graciously revealed himself anew to Simon, as he describes in the beautiful poem that poured out that day in that café, my prayer is that as you read this book, he will do so for you, as he has for me.

RICO TICE
*All Souls Church, Langham Place, London.*

# ACKNOWLEDGEMENTS

A book is always written in collaboration. I am grateful to my publishing team at Muddy Pearl, especially my editor Stephanie Heald, for believing in the project and bringing this beautifully presented book to print during a global pandemic!

I am blessed beyond words to have been a minister at St Aldates, Oxford for over two decades where this material was wrestled with and taught; and for the saints there who have faithfully prayed and encouraged me through this project.

To my friends David and Ruth White for the repeated gift of their beautiful cottage where a weary minister found rest, and where one Easter week, each morning at dawn, this book came together.

Lastly, and firstly, to my wife Tiffany who has always been there and taught me more of Jesus than anyone else. She amazes me.

# CONTENTS

# HE TURNS WATER
# INTO WINE

One Sunday evening at church, I was given a bottle of wine by a friend as a gift. I slipped it into the pocket of my long winter coat, and after church, as was my custom then, went for a kebab for my supper. In the takeaway, there was a group of paratroopers who had just earned their wings at jump school in nearby Brize Norton. Their boisterous behaviour and volume suggested they had been celebrating hard for some time. When they saw my clerical collar they began to mock me. I commented to one rather short, rather vociferous Scottish terrier, 'You're a bit of a bulldog,' at which point the atmosphere instantly changed. The men sobered up.

'Uh oh', I thought, 'now what?'

Then, rolling up his T-shirt, the Scotsman presented a large and colourful tattoo of a bulldog – it was his nickname! I had their attention. A tall, northern paratrooper said, 'Hey, Padre, I bet you can't turn water into wine.' The lads laughed as I reached into my coat pocket and pulled out the bottle of red given to me at church earlier – I held it up and said, 'That was water a minute ago.' I now had a captive audience and could introduce them to Jesus, who really did turn water into wine.

Yes, Jesus really did turn water into wine, but this was no conjuring trick to deceive drunk revellers; this was a demonstration of his character and his power. Jesus was at a local wedding, and the guests had finished off the wine. In Ancient Near Eastern culture, all and sundry were invited to wedding parties – which often lasted for days – and it was the duty of the host to provide a feast. To run out of food or wine was to bring great shame and dishonour on the family, and it would be a disastrous way to begin married life together. Mary, Jesus' mum, was attentive to the problem, and she cared enough to interfere. She knew there was only one person who could sort it out. And so she went, as a mother, to tell her son to do something.

Until this point, the Biblical witness suggests Jesus has worked no miracles. Later Gnostic texts invent absurd tales of the boy Jesus making birds from clay, but Jesus does no miracle until his public ministry begins. But cometh the hour cometh the mum. I love that the woman who bore the eternal *logos* in her womb, who birthed Jesus into the world, would initiate his first public miracle. And what a miracle it was.

There were six giant water jars standing there – probably those used for Jewish ritual washing – and Jesus requested that these be filled with water. And they were. Six jars, each holding twenty to thirty gallons – that's a lot of water! Around a hundred and fifty gallons of water went in. And that was it. No hocus pocus, no nights of passionate intercession, no pleading and beseeching, no promises and vows, no fasting and forsaking. Just: 'Fill the jars with water,' then an immediate 'now draw it out and take it to the master of the feast.' Water went in, wine came out. And when the master of the banquet tastes the wine, he is confused, he cannot believe what he is tasting. So he calls the bridegroom, 'Has there been some sort of mistake?' He says, 'Everyone serves the good wine first, and when people have drunk freely, then the poor wine. But you have kept the best wine till last.' A hundred and fifty gallons of water went in; 900 bottles of wine came out. It was the best wine, the Grand Cru wine, the Château Pétrus 1982 sort of wine.[*]

---

[*] My paraphrase, but you can read about this miracle in John 2:1–12.

In the film *The Avengers*, Iron Man declares to the other superheroes, 'I'm bringing the party to you', when in fact he's bringing trouble.[1] But in the Gospels, people brought their troubles to Jesus and he brought the party to them. John says this was Jesus' first sign and that it showed his glory – what did it signify? Jesus did it because he was there, because he could, when no one else could, and because he cared.

In 2015, the BBC News magazine carried an article that had a deep impact on me – it was titled 'My 25 years as a Prostitute'. Brenda Myers Powell, born in Chicago, lived in hell. Her mother died when she was a child and she was brought up by her alcoholic grandmother, whose drinking friends started abusing her at the age of five. She began prostituting herself at fourteen, when her grandmother sent her out to bring some money in for groceries. And for the next twenty-five years she had sex with five strangers a day. 'These are not relationships, no one's bringing me any flowers here ... they're using my body like a toilet,' she writes. She began using drugs to cover the pain. And yet her 'clients' were not content just to use her sexually; violence was normative, and she was shot five times and stabbed thirteen. One fateful day, her dress caught in the door of a client's car as he drove off, and he dragged her along the road for six blocks – ripping swathes of skin off her face and back. She was taken to the hospital emergency room, and she tells of her experience there:

> They called in a police officer, who looked me over and said: 'Oh I know her. She's just a hooker. She probably beat some guy and took his money and got what she deserved.' And I could hear the nurse laughing along with him. They pushed me out into the waiting room as if I wasn't worth anything, as if I didn't deserve the services of the emergency room after all. And it was at that moment, while I was waiting for the next shift to start and for someone to attend to my injuries, that I began to think about everything that had happened in my life. I remember looking up and saying to God, 'These people don't care about me. Could you please help me?'[2]

And? 'God worked real fast', she said. A doctor came, tended her wounds, contacted the social services, and by the end of the day Brenda entered a woman's refuge called Genesis House. Genesis means beginnings – and for her this was a new beginning. They told her to take her time and stay as long as she needed.

She remembers, 'My face healed. My soul healed.' Brenda went on to found and direct her own charity and ministry helping sex workers and bringing hope and transformation. She became the first woman in the state of Illinois to have her convictions for prostitution wiped from her record.

Water into wine, and Jesus saved the best wine till last.

Maybe your life feels like you have run out of wine. Or maybe the wine of your life has turned to brackish dishwater. In this book I want to show you that Jesus is there, and Jesus cares, and Jesus can make a difference. He can turn it all around – it's what he does.

He is amazing.

SIMON PONSONBY
*Oxford 2020*

# CHAPTER 1

# HE IS AMAZING

*And people who heard him were amazed*
*and some afraid and some angry*

*I have never lost the wonder of it all.*
GYPSY SMITH[3]

After thirty years in ministry I was worn out. I am married to a wonderful wife and have two remarkable grown sons; I serve with a gifted team, in an inspiring and influential church. I have published a number of books, and am invited to speak in numerous contexts at home and abroad. But ministry had sucked the life out of me.

I felt bruised, jaded with much of church life, disappointed at the drift in my denomination, sad at seeing friends and former role models falling into serious moral failure, doctrinal error or throwing in the towel on church. After years of longing and praying and preaching for church renewal and national revival, it seemed further away than ever.

I was not aware of any glaring sin in my own life, but God seemed distant and I was becoming apathetic and cynical. I didn't like what I saw in me. I was spiritually dry, and physically tired, and mentally anxious and depressed. Always an introvert, the strain of public ministry had much reduced me, and I was increasingly withdrawing from company. I snatched comfort in eating and drinking a little too much and hiding myself in my hobbies. I spent more time with the latter than with the Lord. I was not in a good place – all the while, with more desperation than faith, I was calling out to God for help, for change.

In March 2019 I attended the funeral of evangelist and theologian Michael Green. I first came across Michael when I became a Christian thirty-five years ago. I was discipled and equipped by many of his books. Years later I got to know him personally in Oxford. He did me the great honour of writing a beautiful foreword for my first book, *More*.[4]

Michael was one of the outstanding evangelical church leaders of the last forty years and his contribution, through hundreds of missions and over seventy books, is unquestionable and almost unparalleled in his generation. But what struck me at his funeral, as I listened to the contributions and testimonies, was that this man was ablaze with the love for Jesus. It was this love for Jesus that made him such an infectious and effective evangelist.

At the age of 88, he was still passionately preaching Jesus on student missions, still witnessing to the hospital staff nursing him, still handing out booklets that he had written about Jesus to strangers. He was all about Jesus. And people wanted to know the Jesus they saw and encountered in him.

Michael's single-minded focus moved me and, indeed, provoked me. Had I become so caught up in working for the Lord that I had lost the Lord of the work? Probably. Martha was dutifully preoccupied with many things for Jesus, but neglected 'what is better': the option her sister Mary took by sitting and gazing on Jesus. I knew I needed to begin again at the beginning, and return to my first love, Jesus.

Three decades ago, I became a minister because I had met Jesus and he transformed my life and I wanted to tell the world about him. Somewhere that vision of Jesus became blurred, and the ministry had bizarrely pushed Jesus to the periphery.

No longer.

An evangelist of an earlier generation, Gypsy Smith, once said of Jesus: 'I have never lost the wonder of it all.'

I don't ever want to either.

And many haven't. Many are still in that place where they are overwhelmed with Jesus and what he has done for them. But for others of us, there are times when it is as if Jesus is taken from us into the clouds and he appears to be somewhat distant. And many of us face times of attrition in life, periods of intense temptation to sin, or disappointment in the church, or spiritual inertia, or just plain weariness. And in these times we can drift away from the Lord, from our first love. It's as if Jesus no longer thrills us like he once did.

Some of us feel sometimes more 'bored again' than 'born again' believers. One work of the Spirit is to woo our hearts and minds back to Jesus – to shine the spotlight on him and to cause us to be re-captivated by Jesus and to recalibrate our lives around Jesus.

Spiritual author Philip Yancey described it like this,

> For me Jesus has become the focal point of faith, and increasingly I am learning to keep the magnifying glass of my faith focused on him. In my spiritual journey I have long lingered in the margins, puzzling over matters like the problem of pain, the conundrum of prayer, providence versus free will. When I do so, everything becomes fuzzy. Looking at Jesus, however, restores clarity.[5]

In this book I want us to look again at Jesus and where things have got fuzzy, to restore the clarity of our vision of him.

It is said that the Renaissance master Michelangelo was asked by his pupil Raphael to comment on a portrait of Jesus that he was painting. Michelangelo went to his studio to see the picture when Raphael was out for lunch, and after examining the portrait, took a brush and painted across it the word *AMPLIUS* – amplify, make Jesus bigger, larger, make more of Jesus. There's always so much more to know, to learn, to love about Jesus.

Reading Mark's Gospel one day, I was struck by the response of the disciples to Jesus. They had been with him day and night for three years. They had seen his mind-boggling signs and wonders, healings and miracles. They had heard him utter the most profound teaching, and they had observed him live the most perfect life. Familiarity and proximity to this sublime life had bred only wonderment – Jesus never ceased to amaze them. Every day with him brought something new to cause their eyes to pop and their mouths to drop. I think they spent most of their time with their jaws aching, because their mouths were wide open in wonder at this amazing Jesus. Three times in the space of nine short verses, Mark tells us the disciples continued to be amazed and astonished: they were *amazed* by his teaching about the rich young ruler; they were *astonished* as he strode out ahead of them to Jerusalem, his face set like flint.*

In modern use, the word amazing has become somewhat overused and devalued. Everything is now amazing: the latest Netflix series, that new restaurant that has just opened up, the latest wonder-working pain-free diet, England's Rugby team, each successive new fashion, that *Strictly Come Dancing* competitor's foxtrot: it's simply 'A-Ma-Zing'. I was watching that classic blokey programme, *The Great British Sewing Bee,* and as she sent home the weakest contestant the judge said, 'You have been amazing'. And I thought 'Well, why are you sending them home then?' If they were amazing, why send them home? The fact was they weren't amazing; they were rather weak, and everything they put together was falling apart. The zips wouldn't zip up. They were a bit weak. Not amazing. We overuse the word amazing. And when we come to Scripture, we need to think *amazing*. Like, really amazing.

When people ask me how I'm doing, I sometimes reply 'medium'. And people ask why; they think I'm a bit miserable. A bit of an Eeyore.** Can't you be more upbeat? How are you? 'Amazing! Awesome!?' Well I'm not. There are some words that I reserve for special occasions and for special people. And amazing is one I reserve for my wife Tiffany, my two sons, and yes, my favourite

---

* Mark 10:24; 10:26; 10:32.
** Eeyore is the depressive donkey in the tale of Winnie-the-Pooh.

curry at my favourite restaurant. But supremely and pre-eminently, of course, amazing is reserved for Jesus. He is the amazing one.

The Gospel writer Mark uses two different words to convey the sense of amazement – and actually both appear five times, ten times in all. And both convey a sense of a physical response to what they are seeing and hearing. One word is *thambeo* – from the Greek root *tremon* from which we get our word 'to tremble'. When it says they were amazed, it is with this sense of trembling. The other word is *ekpliso*, and it means to strike with a blow. It is translated 'they were amazed', but it means: 'They had the senses knocked out of them.' They were overwhelmed; literally, Jesus knocked them sideways, and he does that.

When we truly see him, when we encounter him and when we comprehend who he is and what he has done for us, there is a sense that we are knocked sideways, flabbergasted, astonished, poleaxed, overwhelmed … or in modern idiom: mind-blown. Mild interest about Jesus shows you've not yet met him. Jesus is amazing.

It was shortly after Michael's funeral, and I was meditating on the Gospels and saw how the response to Jesus from those who met him was *amazement*. As I pondered this, Jesus presented himself afresh to me. Words tumbled out as I sat in a café, tears rolling down my face trying to capture what I was seeing – just how amazing Jesus is.[6]

## JESUS IS AMAZING

*Consider these things:*

*He reigned divine in unapproachable light and incomparable glory*
*He created all things and kept them going by his powerful word*
*He was endlessly worshipped and adored by myriad upon myriad*
*of angels*

*He overflowed in restless love and created humans in his image to love*
*He created a paradise and gave himself to us in a garden of delights*
*He gave us free will so that we might love him back in freedom*
*He did not turn away when we turned away but kept advancing toward us, open armed*
*He covered our nakedness and shame*
*He never gave up on us, never rejected us, never stopped loving us*
*He chased us through the corridors and contours of history*
*He revealed himself in creation and conscience, in words and wonders*
*He chose his servant Israel to reveal his glory to the world*
*He graced us with sacrifice and temple and law so we could stand before him*
*He planned and prophesied and prepared his particular coming to us*
*He is amazing*

*He wed himself to human flesh in virgin womb –*
*He took upon himself our very nature so he might give his nature to us*
*He dwelt among us, one of us, and 'drank the earthly cup to its lees'*[7]
*And aged thirty, he left obscurity, and began his public ministry*
*And he spoke as no man ever spoke before*
*And people who heard him were amazed and some afraid and some angry*
*And he called people to leave all and follow him*

*And he said he was bringing the kingdom of God*
*And he showed us he was the king of the kingdom*
*And he showed us that his was a kind kingdom*
*And he showed us that his was a powerful kingdom where lives were transformed*
*And he gave us the keys of the kingdom*

*And he forgave the sins of the adulterous woman and the cripple who got up and walked*
*And he tenderly touched the leper and healed their skin and removed*

*their shame*
*And he bent double with compassion at the suffering he saw in others*
*And he raised the dead boy and gave him back to his mother*
*And he raised the dead girl and gave her back to her father*
*And he raised his dead friend, and gave him back to his sisters*
*And he opened the eyes of the blind and he opened ears of the deaf*
*And he opened the prisons of the tormented*
*And he opened the minds of the questioning*
*And he opened the way for us to God*
*Now that is amazing*

*And he fed 5000 hungry pilgrims with five small loaves and two fish*
*And he commanded the wind and waves to obey him and they did*
*And he ordered the shadows to depart and they did*
*And he taught us to pray to God as Father*
*And he called his disciples his friends*
*And he had a special heart for society's outcasts*
*And he was transfigured and revealed in all his glory*
*And he wept at the tomb of his friend*
*And he was homeless with nowhere to lay his head*
*And he made friends with tax collectors and sinners and betrayers*
*And he loved the rich young ruler who loved his money more than God*
*And he turned over the tables in the temple to stop the money-changers ripping off the poor*
*And he prayed for us to know God's love and protection and to see his glory*
*And he gave us bread and wine to join with him and with one another*

*Oh, he is amazing*
*And he intimidated the authorities – and he provoked his enemies*
*And wicked men and evil spirits conspired to kill him*
*And he faced down the fear and embraced his destiny for us*
*And he welcomed the betrayer with a kiss, and still called him friend*
*And he did it all willingly, of his own volition, because he loved us*

*And scheming men sat in judgment on him*
*And they condemned him and handed him over*
*And they spat on him and beat him and mocked him, and nailed*
*him and killed him*
*And he took it all, as a willing ransom for our sins*
*And he who knew no sin became sin for us*
*And God laid on him the iniquity of us all*
*And he entered god-forsakenness for our sake*
*And by his stripes we are healed*
*And he drenched the earth with his blood, not anyone else's*
*And he washed us whiter than snow*
*And his executors said 'Truly, this man was the son of God'*

*And they laid him in a stone cold tomb*
*And he descended to the depths*
*And he preached freedom to the prisoners*
*And he set the captives free*
*And he shattered the bonds of death*
*And he had the last word as he pushed the stone away*
*And he cancelled the debt of sin*
*And he satisfied the justice of God*
*And he redeemed us from death and hell*
*And he disarmed the demonic*
*And he brought us home from exile*
*Isn't he just amazing?*

*And ascended to heaven to sit beside the Father in our stead*
*And there he prays for us all day and all night*
*And he sent us his Spirit's power to be with us forever*
*And he asks for nothing from us but faith and love*
*And he placed us in a family*
*And he sent us out to tell others of his love*
*And he is praying for us – right now*
*And he is coming back to be with us*
*And he will judge the living and the dead*
*And he will wipe away all our tears; and drive away our fears and*

*heal our wounded years*
*And he will fully finally vanquish all evil*
*And he will make all things right*

*Meanwhile he's still healing, still cleansing, still delivering, still inviting*
*And today two billion follow him – and many millions suffer for faith*
*And one day the whole earth will be covered with his glory*
*And he is called Jesus – which means God saves us – and he does*
*And he is Emmanuel – which means God is here for us*
*And he is The Lord – he is God over us*
*Yes, he is amazing.*

✝

How can we capture Niagara Falls in an egg cup? We can't! Far less can our human words capture and convey Jesus. We are left with aching jaws – in awe, amazement and wonderment. The agnostic physicist Albert Einstein once claimed,

I am a Jew, but I am enthralled by the luminous figure of the Nazarene. Jesus is too colossal for the pen of phrasemongers, however artful.[8]

I am just a phrasemonger, but I don't ever cease to be amazed by Jesus. In the words of that old hymn,

I stand amazed in the presence
of Jesus the Nazarene,
and wonder how he could love me,
a sinner condemned, unclean.[9]

The saintly Victorian Oxford scholar Edward Pusey said of such things as stated here,

> It surpasses all thought, it amazes, it confounds, to think of God becoming man; the Infinite enshrined within the finite ... the Creator with His creature! It is a depth of mystery unsearchable. We must shrink with awe when we pronounce it.[10]

We must shrink with awe when we pronounce it – and then run to embrace it.

In Donald Miller's spiritual journal, *Blue Like Jazz*, he tells of a friend of his, Alan, who was researching 'successful' churches and interviewing their leaders. Alan travelled across the USA asking pastors why they were doing what they were doing. He visited Bill Bright, one of the most influential Christian leaders of the twentieth century, founder of Campus Crusade for Christ that has about 25,000 missionaries in 200 countries. Alan was shown into a rather grand office and there behind a big desk was the big man himself. Alan asked various questions and then finished with this: 'What does Jesus mean to you?' And Bill Bright just started to cry. 'He sat there in a big chair behind his big desk and wept.' Donald Miller comments,

> When Alan told me the story I wondered what it was like to love Jesus that way. To cry at the very mention of the name Jesus ... I knew then, I would like to know Jesus like that.[11]

Me too.

Maybe there was a time when you did thrill, or fill with tears at the mention of his name – come back to that place again, come back to him. Or maybe you've never met him – today, right now, come to him, talk to him now, and give yourself to him – just as you are, say,

*'Jesus, you are amazing, I am yours.'*

# CHAPTER 2

# HE IS HOME

*He dwelt among us, one of us*

*How lovely is your dwelling-place,*
*Lord Almighty!*
*My soul yearns, even faints,*
*for the courts of the Lord;*
PSALM 84:1–2

Every year I look forward to the Christmas adverts. This annual festive tradition in the UK calls on the talents of gifted creatives and they really do produce some great storytelling. One recent standout was a supermarket advert which was set inside someone's 'imaginarium', where strapping blokes with long moustaches in tight green leotards were smashing sugar-ice-igloos with great big sledgehammers. I thought it was … very interesting, although perhaps more Freudian regression than Holy Nativity. It is also interesting how few of these Christmas adverts actually cover traditional Christmas themes. Instead we have Mog the Cat, Buster the Dog, Monty the Penguin, and Moz the Monster, and the children's favourite, Kevin the Carrot.

It's also interesting how few adverts promote actual products. Especially given that all this advertising does come at some cost – they spent some 4 billion pounds last year. Perhaps the advertising executives know we would be disappointed, would feel we were being sold short? After all, it's not really things that we want at Christmas, is it? I believe that they understand that – they don't have the solution, they don't have the answer, but they recognize the deep longing that is in the human heart, and they tug at that. Most commercials appeal to sentiment, they convey feeling, emotion, a sense of nostalgia, and try to hint that they can meet something of that longing.

## AT CHRISTMAS, THE WORLD IS LONGING FOR HOME

And what is it that we long for? I believe we all long for home, especially at Christmas, there is a sort of universal homing device in our soul at Christmas time. Each year Bing Crosby's famous song comes out, *'I'll be home for Christmas'* and everyone's nostalgia for home is rekindled. This song was recorded in 1943 to encourage American Troops, the GIs serving away from home, fighting on the European and Pacific fronts. With that typical British spirit of 'Bah! Humbug!', the BBC banned the song because they felt it might lower morale, and make the troops homesick. Home for Christmas is a meme that is widely repeated – each year animal charities remind us to 'give a dog a home for Christmas'. I love dogs, although I think a home for the hundreds of thousands of people who are homeless, sleeping rough or living in temporary accommodation might be a more pressing need.[12]

For several years, Coca-Cola have re-released an adaptation of a particularly successful advert first made in 1995, of a convoy of red trucks lit up with Christmas lights arriving in a snow-covered town, to a song that is rising in speed and volume: 'Holidays are coming, holidays are coming, holidays are coming!' Coca-Cola then began organising tours, so that people could get a free Coke and have their photo taken next to the iconic trucks. We all look forward to Christmas, because it is a holiday, but a holiday is not enough.

One year, my boss gave me Christmas off – imagine that, a priest having Christmas off! I was thrilled. Some friends from church offered us their Cornish cottage over the holiday, and so we packed our bags and went to spend the holiday away. But after just three days I noticed Tiffany was a bit quiet. And so I said, 'What's wrong love?' and Tiffany said, 'This just isn't Christmas. I want Christmas at home.' I said, 'But we're on holiday.' And she said 'I know, but I want to go home.' So we took down our decorations, packed the car, and drove home. We were back in time to be with our church family for midnight communion. And my boss very graciously gave me the opportunity to work.

But what is it about Christmas and home? What is this nostalgia for? Is it tapping into memories from the past, happy childhood memories of good food and being spoiled? Is it the family reunions? Is it the chance to have a rest from work? Or is it a deep knowing that Christmas marks the longest point of winter, and that from now on the nights will grow shorter?[13] Perhaps it is all of that – but also more than that.

American spiritual writer Frederick Buechner insightfully claimed that when we hear the word 'home' we think of two things: we think of the place we come from and we think of the place we dream of.[14] I think that is very true. But these two places, these two homes are not the same. The home we come from cannot meet the need or satisfy the longing for the home we dream of. Just as the anticipation of, say, a Christmas cracker, is rarely fulfilled – it never quite goes bang, the paper hat never fits, invariably tears and always looks silly, on me anyway, the joke is never all that funny, and that plastic bat ring is not your thing – so, going home for Christmas, however good, is never the homecoming you hope for. We are always left wanting more.

Priest and poet, Pádraig Ó Tuama, in his moving spiritual autobiography, expresses his, and our, search to find home. These lines put into words what so many so often feel as deep aches inside:

I yearn for home

I've heard that Elves
Have ships on which to sail away,

Across the morning waters
To their grey havens
Fair and far away
From here.

I wonder if all my longings
Could shape for me
A ship of hopes
To carry me
On these seas of homeward yearning
I yearn for home[15]

This longing is our soul's homing device for God. You see, we are made by God, like God, for God, we are wired for him – we have a nostalgia for God. The home we seek is with him. Gifted Korean writer RO Kwon, author of *The Incendiaries*, has written about her rejection of belief in God. Far from being a liberation from ignorance and control, she admits that now,

> I know such a lot about being afraid. Just to glance at the news is to spin into the kind of anxiety that leaves me awake all night, as though, by fretting … but standing up to these fears wouldn't solve the underlying problems. I miss God so much. It's a hole cut out of me, a loss that's always there.[16]

We are made for God, and our hearts are restless till they find their rest in him, claimed the fourth century theologian, Augustine of Hippo, but he understated it. Restless? More like desperate. That loss of God will only be satisfied when we come to the home we dream of with God. Only God can satisfy our longing for God.

The psalmist writes of a similar longing for home:

> *How lovely is your dwelling-place,*
> *Lord Almighty!*
> *My soul yearns, even faints,*
> *for the courts of the Lord;*

*my heart and my flesh cry out*
*for the living God.*
*Even the sparrow has found a home,*
*and the swallow a nest for herself,*
*where she may have her young –*
*a place near your altar,*
*Lord Almighty, my King and my God.*
*Blessed are those who dwell in your house;*
*they are ever praising you.*

PSALM 84:1–4

At Christmas we all long for home, but the question is, where is that home? The psalmist says even the sparrow has found a home near God's altar. He'd been to Jerusalem, he'd been to the temple, he'd perhaps seen a nest and he'd seen a sparrow, and he knew that the sparrow was near the presence of God in Israel. And there was a longing in his heart to be near God. There was a longing of this pilgrim to be home.

That first Christmas, the three wise men left the home they came from to find the home they dreamed of. Tradition, rather than the Bible, says there were three wise men, presumably because there were three named gifts given to Jesus' parents: gold, frankincense and myrrh. Tradition has also given the wise men names: Balthazar, Caspar and Melchior. The last time I went to Israel was just before Christmas, to teach a conference. As we boarded the plane, over the intercom came the captain's voice: 'Would Mr and Mrs Melchior please report to a steward' – 'Whoa,' I thought, 'I'm in the story! Pilgrimage!' In Jerusalem I stayed inside the walled Old City on the site of Herod's palace where some 2000 years earlier the wise men made their pilgrimage to worship the King. They went to the palace because they knew a king had been born, and they thought obviously he's been born in a palace, so there they went. The wise men went to the wrong place and nearly got Jesus murdered – so they weren't all *that* wise after all then. It's claimed that had they been three wise women, they would have asked directions, arrived on time, helped deliver the baby, swept the stable, made a casserole and brought practical gifts. Their timing was right, but their direction a couple of miles off – Jesus, whom they sought was about six miles away in Bethlehem.

How often do we look for the king in the wrong place – for God in the wrong place – for home in the wrong place?

Some suggest these wise men or *Magi*, from the Greek word *magoi*, were Zoroastrian occultists from Persia (Iran). Others have suggested they were astrologers from Babylon (Iraq). The text simply speaks of 'wise men from the East'* who saw a special star rise and believed the prophecies about a king to be born, come to rule the world, the longing of the ages was going to be fulfilled in Jerusalem.

Now if the *Magi* came from Iraq then they journeyed over five hundred miles from their home. If they came from Iran they journeyed over a thousand miles. Such extraordinary lengths to come – whether they came on foot or in a camel caravan or on horseback. But there is a fascinating document that has recently come to light in the Vatican archives. It's an eighth century document, itself a copy of a much earlier second century document, held in the Vatican library, and it is the longest account of the visit of the wise men. It suggests that these mysterious mystical *Magi* came much, much farther. The document tells of a caravan of wise men, that followed a star along the silk route, to Israel, from the land of *Shir*. *Shir* is the ancient name associated with China.[17] If the *Magi* did come from China, they journeyed for at least 5000 miles – well over a year on pilgrimage.

The wise men left the home they came from to find the home they dreamed of. The wise men followed the star, followed the prophecies, followed their hearts and followed the road to Jerusalem and to Jesus. And the hopes and fears of all their years were met in him that night.

---

* Matthew 2:1.

The wise men found what they were looking for, not in a king's palace, but in an animals' manger – where the bread of life was laid. God with us, God like us, God for us. What a journey, what a conclusion – no wonder the Gospel records: 'they rejoiced exceedingly with great joy'* and gave gifts and worshipped him. When you find the home you have always dreamed of, and meet God, you overflow with joy and worship and give your life and all to him. Some reading this have been on a long journey, for a long time, looking for home. Most people spend all their lives on this journey and few find home. Home is where Jesus is.

## THAT FIRST CHRISTMAS, JESUS LEFT THE HOME HE CAME FROM TO MAKE THE ONE WE DREAMED OF

St John the Beloved wrote, 'the Word became human and made his *home* among us'.** What an extraordinary thing. All the other noble religions say that you get yourself right and ready for God. But Christian faith says God came to us, and he made us right for him. And it's a long way from there to here. It's a long way from *Deus* to *foetus*. It's a long way from heaven to earth. It's a long way from Lord of the universe to dependent little child. It's a long way from eternal glory to dirty nappies. Jesus made that long journey willingly. Jesus journeyed a long way from home to make his home with us. It was a costly journey that would lead to his rejection, suffering and death.

One Christmas advert by a high end supermarket stands out to me – it tells the story of Robin Redbreast, who goes on a perilous journey, across snowy mountains and stormy seas and faces dangerous predators. Finally, wearily, he arrives in a garden where another red robin is waiting. (And a mince pie, which is always useful.)

*Matthew 2:10–11 (ESV).
**John 1:14 (NLT).

That first Christmas, Jesus made that long perilous journey. He crossed oceans, mountains, through time and space from eternity and glory, through incarnation and vulnerability to be with us in our humanity on that first Christmas day and ever thereafter.

But why would he do this? Simply and unfathomably, because he loved us. Jesus wanted to make his home with us and he would go through hell and high water to make this possible. That baby in a crib will become a man on a cross – and his death will end death and unlock the gate to Eden, paradise, heaven's garden, barred since the fall of our first parents who sinned and were exiled. It is there with God that our hearts long for, that is the home God destined for us.

Over thirty years ago I was living in Bristol, working in the wholesale meat trade. It was a very demanding job, a lot of responsibility, I was working sixty-hour weeks – often starting before five in the morning, after walking through the city to work. I was not looking after myself, not sleeping well, not eating properly and began to become ground down. I was on the edge of a physical if not mental breakdown. One night I rang my parents at 2am for a chat. At 2am! My dad instantly sensed something was wrong – you don't ring for a chat at 2am, or at least I didn't. Dad hung up – the line went dead. 'Nice', I thought. My parents lived twelve miles away. But half an hour later, there was a knock at the door – it was my mum – stood there in a pink dressing gown, on my doorstep. 'Get in the car son, I'm taking you home'. She ordered. 'No Mum, I'm just off to work' I protested. 'Get in the car,' she replied. I did – she handed me a drink and some tablets – I woke twelve hours later, in my old bedroom, in my old bed, back home. Dad told me Mum had driven back into Bristol and spoken to my boss and quit my job, for me. Rest and recovery and a new direction in work and life came after that.

What is Jesus like? Who is Jesus? He is like this: a God who came to us, making a perilous journey across oceans and mountains, time and space. He came like us, he came for us, not in a pink dressing gown, but in swaddling clothes. And he keeps coming, and keeps knocking on the door of our heart saying, 'I've come to take you home'.

Where are you looking for Jesus?

# CHAPTER 3

# HE IS READY

*He planned and prophesied and prepared his particular
coming to us*

*But when the set time had fully come, God sent his Son,
born of a woman*
GALATIANS 4:4

I love the excitement and anticipation of Christmas. All that
preparation: all that budgeting, ordering of food, buying of gifts,
sending out of cards and of annual family news, collecting and
dressing the tree, arranging visits, organizing the break, dieting
in advance, booking the hairdresser before, booking the gym
membership for afterwards, and decorating the house. Although
without taking that last one too far – the most bizarre advice on
preparing for Christmas I have come across advised:

> In October, with twelve weeks to go, it's time to start considering
> your Christmas décor. Get into the festive spirit by taking some
> time out to browse different festive trends and styles. Embracing
> this season's leopard prints? You'll adore the wilderness trend.
> Prefer a traditional look? Winter bloom is for you.[18]

Yes, I do prefer a traditional look, but not 'winter bloom'! Our
materialist culture, or perhaps it's our materialist nature, has
turned advent into adverts. Three years ago, on Christmas Day in
the UK, £1billion was spent online shopping – on Christmas Day
itself! Something has gone seriously wrong. I am reminded of Bart

Simpson's ironic comment: 'Aren't we forgetting the true meaning of Christmas … you know … the birth of Santa.'[19]

Advent is meant to be an adventure with God. The word is a conjunction of two Latin words: come (*venio*) and to (*ad*), giving *advenio*, meaning to arrive or reach, but in ancient Rome this word also had a sense of a 'glorious entry' of an emperor into the city. Advent is a time when we celebrate God coming to us. We come to the God who has come to us.

On Haven Today's blog, Ann Voskamp writes,

> We're ready for Christmas, not when we have all the gifts, but when we are ready for Christ – when we're ready to give all of ourselves to Christ.[20]

Exactly. And we should be preparing to meet God every day of the year.

## GOD PREPARED TO MEET US

No one looked forward to Christmas more than God. Aeons in the planning, God set his heart and mind on coming and dwelling among us, on loving and giving himself to us, on redeeming and reconciling all humankind to himself. And all this through the birth of Jesus. The Gospel birth narratives reveal a meticulous divine choreography. There were no accidentals or incidentals – God was sovereignly working out his purpose and plan. He prepared every detail.

## GOD PREPARED THE MOMENT

The timing of the arrival of Jesus was perfect. The Apostle Paul wrote, 'when the set time had fully come, God sent his Son' (eternal, divine) 'born of a woman' (temporal, human) and again, 'at just the right time … Christ died for the ungodly'.[*]

---

[*] Galatians 4:4; Romans 5:6.

External wars followed by internal internecine conflicts occupied the Roman Empire for centuries and would eventually bring her decline through the fourth century and collapse in the fifth. But there was a brief window in history when there was relative calm, a lull across the Empire, a golden era: peace under Julius Augustus lasted for just a few decades before and after Jesus' birth. Monuments were erected around the time of the birth of Christ celebrating this *Pax Augusta*. Everyone was talking about peace on earth – the Roman poets declared Augustus 'the saviour of the world, good news for the world, bringer of world peace'.[21] Sound familiar? And at just the right time, God sends his Son, announced by angels heralding 'good news of great joy'[*]: a Saviour of the world, a Prince of Peace, has come.

The famed Roman historian Tacitus tells us that Augustus showed unprecedented zeal for an empire-wide census, surveys and stocktaking. And at just the right time, 'Caesar Augustus issued a decree that a census should be taken of the entire Roman world'[**] and the whole Empire was on the move to get one Holy Family to the prophesied birthplace of kings at the right time to fulfil God's promises and plans. At just the right time, in a unique window in history when Greek was a unifying and universalizing language, when the legal- and military-supported *Pax Romana* secured all national frontiers for trade and safe passage, when roads were built and routes established for easy travel, at just that right time came God's Son, and came the Gospel which could be broadcast to the world.

## GOD PREPARED THE ENVIRONMENT

Following the Emperor's decree, Joseph takes his betrothed, Mary, to register in Bethlehem, home of his ancestors. Bethlehem is both the birthplace of King David and where the king was crowned. Five

[*] Luke 2:10 (ESV).
[**] Luke 2:1.

hundred years before Christ's birth the prophets foretold that one day the King of kings would be born there.[*]

*Beth'lehem* in Hebrew means literally the 'house of bread'. In the story of Ruth, the family must leave Israel for Moab due to a famine in the land. But when the famine ends they return to Bethlehem during a harvest time; in Bethlehem they receive bread, new life.[**] It is from Bethlehem that David, a 'type' of Christ, takes ten loaves of bread to his brothers fighting the Philistines and his eventual slaying of the giant Goliath. The British comedian Jo Brand humorously, mocking her own girth, said, 'I was not a particularly small child. I was the one who always got picked to play Bethlehem in the school nativity.'[22] But Bethlehem, the place where kings are born, where giant-slayers are born, where kings are crowned, where bread is found, where famines end, here in the 'house of bread', here, Jesus, bread of heaven, bread of life, is born.

## GOD PREPARED THE PORTENT

The wise men came from the East to Herod and asked 'Where is the one who has been born king of the Jews?' for they had seen his star rise in the East.[***] Suetonias, the first-century Roman historian, wrote, 'There had spread over all the Orient an old and established belief, that it was fated at that time for men coming from Judea to rule the world.'[23] Indeed, as we mentioned earlier, the world was pregnant with expectancy of a king coming to rule it, and the portent – the sign – of this saviour's appearing was to be a star. Pagan history records a star, given the Egyptian name *Mesori*, meaning 'Birth of a Prince', that rose and shone from 5BC to 2BC, just as Jesus was born.

At just the right time, God sent a special guiding light to direct people to the epiphany of the Light of the world.

[*] Luke 2:4; Micah 5:2.
[**] Ruth 2:14.
[***] Matthew 2:2.

## GOD PREPARED THE PARENTS

Why did God choose Mary and her betrothed partner Joseph? Despite the claims of some traditions, neither were perfect, and both would need to be saved through their Son. But the Gospel narratives show them both as extraordinary: spiritual, kind, courageous, humble, attentive to God, faithful, trustworthy. Angels are not given to hyperbole or flattery – God's messenger Gabriel addresses Mary with a telling character reference: 'Greetings, you who are highly favoured! The Lord is with you' (Luke 1:28). I'm no Greek scholar, but I'm told this is in the perfect passive tense and indicates her current status, what she already was: in a state graced by God. Prior to her ever giving her willing consent to have the Son of the Most High conceived within her, a virgin, she was already favoured by God; she walked with God. Mary's gracious *Yes* to God's staggering request shows her as a model of faith, willing to embrace the likely ignominy, rejection and the burden of being a mother, let alone one in such incomprehensible conditions. But her song, the 'Magnificat' (Luke 1:46) shows her theological depth, her familiarity with the Scriptures (there are eighteen Old Testament references in her song), her intimacy with God and her true meekness before him.

The church has made two errors regarding Mary: the first error is to so venerate Mary as to almost worship her, to make her the focus of our devotion, intercession and revelation of God. Indeed, at its worst, the veneration of Mary almost supplants Jesus as mediator and redeemer. The second error, perhaps a reaction to the first, is to ignore her, to exclude her from salvation history, to see her as some surrogate who incubated Jesus.

In his last breaths, from the cross, Jesus said to John, 'Here is your mother.' This mother of the Lord is the mother of the church, the model of discipleship and worthy of utmost honour and love. When Mary's betrothed husband Joseph hears or sees she is pregnant, he could, under the Jewish law, have had her stoned for adultery, let alone apparent blasphemy (claiming to be pregnant by God!). Yet, despite what must have been such a traumatic experience for him, there is no evidence of animosity, self-pity or revenge, being a '*righteous* man' he did not want 'to disgrace her publicly, so he decided to break the engagement quietly'. This is surely a remarkable response from a remarkable man – all this before the angel explained. Joseph's righteousness takes on a whole new meaning here: not a minute observing of the written and oral law, but an act of tenderness and compassion. God entrusted his Son and the redemption to the perfect parents to nurture his eternal Son.

## GOD PREPARED THE CELEBRANTS

During the night watch, through water and blood, Jesus broke into our world. It was a Holy Night but not a Silent Night as a myriad of angels, 'the armies of heaven' suddenly burst through the heavens to blow the minds and ears of the shepherds. Rehearsed for aeons, in unison they all sing 'Glory to God in highest heaven'.[*] I am reminded of the image painted by JRR Tolkien in his remarkable creation myth, *The Silmarillion*, which begins with the universe being 'sung' into being by angelic creatures, the Ainur, who sing the great song, interweaving their own improvised harmonies around the theme God has laid down. Tolkien's divine figure orchestrates these spiritual beings: 'of the theme that I have declared to you, I will now that ye make in harmony together a Great Music'.[24] What a great music was sung that night when God began his recreation of the universe through the incarnation of his Son. Let us not hold back in celebrating the theme God has laid down, by joining in that song, with great music.

The shepherds aren't told, exactly, but seem to know where to go to meet this newborn Messiah. There has been much speculation and commentary about where exactly and in what exactly Jesus

[*] Luke 2:8, 13–14.

was born. A stable, a cave, a back room? The texts do not permit precision. One considered theory is by the Jewish scholar Alfred Edersheim, drawing on Jewish tradition and lore, who suggested that the place Jesus was born was Bethlehem's *Migdal Eder*, the tower which was used to watch over the special sacrificial flocks of the temple from birth to temple sacrifice.[25] At the tower was a stable where ewes delivered the lambs which were then wrapped in swaddling strips. Edersheim offers several important connections:

- *Migdal Eder* (literally 'Tower of the Flock') is mentioned in Genesis 35 as the place where Rachel died giving birth to a son, Benjamin. The name Benjamin means 'Son of my Right Hand', but it wasn't his original name. He was first called Ben-Oni meaning 'Son of Sorrow'. So, there is a connection between *Migdal Eder*, Bethlehem and a child who is both a 'Son of Sorrow' and 'Son of my Right Hand'.
- Micah 4 establishes the expectation of a godly King intrinsically linked with *Migdal Eder* who would ultimately restore God's people and lead them victorious over evil. This Messianic figure would bring ultimate peace because he would establish God's rule among the nations.
- According to Jewish writings, the shepherds of Bethlehem would tend the sheep for the temple sacrifices. In addition, it was said that when a lamb which met the requirements for the Passover sacrifice was born, the shepherd would wrap it in cloth and lay it in a feeding groove on the floor of *Migdal Eder* to prevent it from any harm.

Of course, we cannot be dogmatic, but these details do offer a possible and very beautiful insight into the prophetic planning of this amazing event by God. At just the right time, and in just the right place.

Jesus the Lamb of God is born, wrapped in strips of swaddling, laid in a manger and the Good Shepherd is honoured by Israel's shepherds: the Lamb of God, worshipped by those who provided the lambs of temple sacrifice. Beautiful poetry.

The only other guests were the *wise men.** Noble, scholarly, wealthy – able to bring highly valuable gifts, able to take a break from life and work and pilgrimage for hundreds of miles: 500 if from Iraq, 1000 miles if from Iran, 5000 miles if from China, and noble enough to gain an audience with King Herod. The King of kings is rightly worshipped with gifts fit for a king, by nobles from afar.

## GOD PREPARED THE INFANT

*when Christ came into the world, he said:*
*'Sacrifice and offering you did not desire,*
*But a body you prepared for me;'*

HEBREWS 10:5

Here is the miracle and marvel that is Emmanuel. Almost too wonderful for human comprehension. Incredulous to some – like the first-century Jewish scholar, Philo, who claimed, 'the life to God has not descended to us.'[26] Well, God in the first century proved them wrong. Here, issuing from a virgin womb, comes a life that is the source of life. *Vere Deus vere homo* – God for man, man for God. God contracted to a span, God condescending to kiss man; the eternal Word, divinity and humanity wed in flesh and blood.

In CS Lewis' *The Last Battle*, the children find a stable, like a Tardis: bigger inside than from the outside. Queen Lucy sees, 'Yes, in our world too, a stable once held something inside it that was bigger than our whole world.'[27]

---

* Matthew 2.

✝

The Apostle Paul wrote,

*when the time had fully come, God sent his Son born of woman, born under the law, to redeem those under the law, that we might receive adoption to sonship.*

GALATIANS 4:4–5

At Christmas God's Son (eternal, divine) came, born of woman 'temporal, human', to make us sons of God. Why? Christina Rossetti told us why: 'love came down at Christmas'.[28]

*Finally, having seen God's preparations, are you prepared to come to Jesus?* The portents and the prophets heralded the coming of the King of the universe to be our king; sadly only a few wise men from the East set their hearts on pilgrimage and homage, and only a few shepherds were awake for this heavenly epiphany. Eternity in preparation, divine invitations sent far and wide, but almost everyone missed the royal birth.

But it's actually worse than that – when the wise men came to King Herod and the priests and teachers explained the star's significance and prophesied birth site – rather than a stampede to see this king, we are told that Herod was 'disturbed, and all Jerusalem with him'[*]; they were disturbed, shaken and wanted nothing to do with what God wanted. We read of no pilgrimage of priests and scholars and nobles coming to see this sign – just discomfort at the intrusion of God, and ultimately rejection.

You will be familiar with the Sistine Chapel's remarkable fresco painted by Michelangelo. Most famous is the depiction of God reaching out his right hand to Adam – life at his fingertips. Has this not always been God's desire: to connect to humankind? But Adam has so often clenched his fist and turned away. A generation after the

[*] Matthew 2:3.

famed Michelangelo, another artistic master was born, also named Michelangelo – but to distinguish him from the former, he was known by the name of his hometown: Caravaggio. Like the earlier Michelangelo, he produced a famous painting which also focused on hands – not the creation of man, but the recreation of man through the birth of Jesus. In the painting, Saint Francis of Assisi has his hands clasped in prayer; Jacob (the father of the twelve sons/tribes of Israel) has his old hands leaning on his staff in worship; the angel above has one hand pointing to heaven and one hand pointing to the Christ child; both Mary and Joseph have their hands pointing to Jesus; and the infant Jesus – reaches out his right hand to touch Joseph's toes. The Mafia stole the painting in the 1960s – it remains lost. Someone's always trying to steal Christmas – don't let it be stolen from you: reach out your hands, to God who has reached out his hand, in Jesus.

# CHAPTER 4

# HE IS NOT A WHITE EUROPEAN

*He chose his servant Israel to reveal his glory to the world*

*And at the end of eight days, when he was circumcised, he was called Jesus, the name given by the angel before he was conceived in the womb.*
LUKE 2:21 (ESV)

God became a Jew and the church uncircumcised him.

The powerful movie *In Darkness* is set in Poland during the Second World War and follows the true story of Jews hiding in the sewers and being looked after, initially for money, by a petty-criminal Leopold Socha. In one early scene, Socha and a colleague are eating supper while spewing anti-Semitic bile against the Jews when Socha's wife Wanda expresses some pity for their plight. She is quickly rebuked: 'The Jews crucified Jesus – the priests said so!' implying they deserved all they got. But Wanda answers, 'Our Lady and the Apostles were all Jews. Even Jesus.'

Socha is stunned. Jesus a Jew? What? Socha soon finds more Jewish people hiding in the sewers and then he begins to care for them, even offering to adopt a newborn child. He succeeds in protecting them from the authorities and saving many from certain death in the camps, and he does so at risk of his own life. Israel would subsequently bestow on him the all too rare title of 'Righteous Gentile'.[29]

Shaye Cohen, Littauer Professor of Hebrew Literature and Philosophy at Harvard University writes,

Jesus was a Jew, born in Galilee. Like most of the other inhabitants of the Roman province of Judaea, he worshipped the God whose temple was in Jerusalem. Not only was Jesus a Jew but so were all of his disciples ('Apostles'), all those who gathered to see his miracles or hear his words ('crowds'), and almost all those who benefited from his miraculous cures. As 'king of the Jews' (perhaps 'king of the Judaeans' would be better) he was sentenced to death by the Romans. After his death his followers, all of whom were Jews like Jesus himself, constituted a Jewish movement, perhaps a sect, meeting and praying regularly in the temple of Jerusalem and interacting with other Jewish worshipers. (At least this is the story in the opening chapters of Acts.) And yet before very long the Jesus movement was no longer Jewish; it became something different ...[30]

As the power centre of the church moved from Jerusalem to Rome, as the apostolic leadership of the church moved from Jewish to Gentile, Middle Eastern to Western, so the theology of the church increasingly lost touch with its Jewish roots and embraced the Greco-Roman language, culture and philosophy. The church began to understand itself as not merely fulfilling Judaism, but replacing it, supplanting it, annulling it. Jews increasingly became archetypes of all that is opposed to God: those who killed Christ and persecuted the early church. That the Lord, and his Apostles and the church, were Jewish faded from thought; a sinister anti-Semitic spirit infiltrated the church and has stained her history ever since. Having detached Jewish roots from Christianity, the denouement was to detach Jesus from his Jewishness, making him appear like a long-blonde-haired, blue-eyed, Californian surfer dude.

One is spoilt for choice for blatant and banal ecclesiastical anti-Semitism, but one low mark is the 1939 theological think-tank called 'The Institute for the Study and Elimination of Jewish Influence on German Church Life'.[31] This was established by a group of influential theologians who systematically removed every trace of Jewishness from their New Testament – including such words as Jerusalem, Israel and Jehovah. They posited two preposterous suppositions: 1) Jesus was descended from Persian or Iryan settlers in Galilee and 2) the Persians are related to the same Indo-European peoples as Aryan. Thus, Jesus was not a Jew but Iryan, that is, an Aryan Prince; indeed, an anti-Semite, a proto-Nazi, whose ministry was to crush Judaism and who would die at the hand of the evil Jews. They claimed the Nazi non-Jewish Jesus would support their programmatic pogroms.

The four main motifs of exorcism of the Nazi New Testament – that is, the four main themes they sought to remove – were all themes which demonstrate the importance of the Jewishness of God's Son. They were: prophecy fulfilled, birth narratives, the Passover and the title 'the King of the Jews'.

It strikes me that the devil attacks or derides what most offends him. In this chapter I want to celebrate what the Nazi Bible sought to denigrate.

## JESUS FULFILLED OLD TESTAMENT JEWISH PROPHECY

Judaism is a religion of a book: a book full of prophecy. The long-awaited Jewish Messiah must necessarily fulfill Jewish prophetic expectation. According to the Gospel writers, Jesus did. They repeatedly cite the Old Testament to show how Jesus was the fulfilment of the prophets. Jesus came *when* it was prophesied he would (before the Second Temple was destroyed); Jesus came *where* it was prophesied he would (Bethlehem); Jesus came *how* it was prophesied he would (born of a virgin); Jesus came and did *what* it was prophesied he would do (open the eyes of the blind, heal the lame, open the ears of the deaf) and Jesus came and died in the way it was prophesied he would – rejected, crucified, resurrected.[*]
The New Testament cannot be read without understanding the Old

---

[*] Daniel 9:24–27; Micah 5:2; Isaiah 7:14; Isaiah 35:5–6; Isaiah 53:3; Numbers 21:9; Job 19:23–27.

Testament.

The fourth edition of the *United Bible Societies' Greek New Testament* (1993) lists 343 Old Testament quotations in the New Testament, as well as no fewer than 2,309 allusions and verbal parallels. The Old Testament books most referred to in the New Testament are Psalms (79 quotations, 333 allusions) and Isaiah (66 quotations, 348 allusions). In the Book of Revelation, there are no direct quotations, but it is estimated there are over 600 allusions. Professor of Mathematics and Astronomy, Dr Peter Stoner, estimated that the probability of Jesus fulfilling just 48 of the 350 main prophecies would be 1 to 10 to the power of 157 – the odds are 1 in 10 with 157 noughts. This number defies comprehension.[32]

The impossibility without divine intervention to fulfill such numerous and diverse prophecies vindicates Jesus as the Jewish Messiah.

Messianic Rabbi, Jonathan Bernis, in his presentation of Jesus' fulfillment of Messianic prophecies asks, 'If Jesus is not the Messiah who is?' There are no other candidates. While others have claimed to be the Messiah, as he claimed to be, they cannot meet the prophetic criteria. A few years ago, disciples of one main ultra-Orthodox Rabbi waited for him to rise from the dead – which, of course, he didn't! Jesus did, which is why over 2 billion worship him as Lord today.

Noting that Jesus fulfills many prophecies in great detail, while all other claimants to Messiah have fulfilled almost none, Rabbi Bernis notes three significant prophecies which were not fulfilled by Jesus in his time on earth:

1. the *establishment* of an earthly kingdom on David's throne,
2. the *gathering* to the land of dispersed Jews from the nations,
3. the *bringing* of world peace.

Bernis sees the second of these as having been fulfilled in our day, since 1948 – while the other two await the Messiah's second coming.[33]

## JESUS' VERY JEWISH BIRTH

The very Jewishness of Jesus is firstly seen in his name, Jesus: a Greek form of the Hebrew Joshua or *Jehoshua* which means 'Yahweh saves', or 'the help of *Yahweh*' or '*Yahweh* rescues'. A Hebrew name honouring a Hebrew God who saves Hebrews might just possibly have been given to a Gentile at that time, but it was unlikely. Furthermore, Jesus had an unequivocally Jewish genealogy. The 1982 *Readers' Digest* edition of the Bible vandalized the Jewishness of Jesus by excising what they thought were extraneous bits: the Matthaen and Lukan Biblical genealogies. They foolishly thought this would make reading the Gospels easier, even though it clouded the reader's ability to digest who Jesus was. However, in living memory, the Nazi theologians removed the genealogies of Jesus, not to make reading easier, but to obliterate the clear testimony they give to Jesus' very real and ancient Jewish lineage. To any Jewish person this act was sacrilege, an assault on one's very being. Jewish genealogies are Jewish DNA profiles that serve to record and legitimate Jewishness. In the two Gospel genealogies they show unequivocally that Jesus had a birthright to both kingly and priestly lines.

Matthew's Genealogy* shows the 'Royal Line' of Jesus through Joseph (his legal father), which follows forty Jewish generations from Abraham, and the legal line of kingship from David.

Luke's Genealogy** shows the 'real line' of Jesus through his natural mother Mary – tracing seventy-five generations back to Adam.

In the remarkable testimony of Messianic Rabbi Mordechai Mottel Baleston[34] (who was raised an ultra-Orthodox Jew) we hear

---

* Matthew 1:1–16.
** Luke 3:23–38.

how his eyes were opened in a library when reading the opening of the New Testament beginning at Matthew. He realized immediately what it asserted: Jesus is Israel's Messiah, the son of David, the son of Abraham. It couldn't get more Jewish than that. Rabbi Baleston was totally overwhelmed by this – he says that growing up in New York the only Christians he had ever met were Italian Catholics so he assumed that Jesus was Italian! Messianic theologian Arnold Fruchtenbaum has written,

> As the Seed of the woman, Messiah had to come out of humanity. As the Seed of Abraham, Messiah had to come from the nation of Israel. As the Seed of Judah, he had to be of the tribe of Judah. As the Seed of David, he had to be of the family of David.[35]

And the Gospels show how Jesus fulfilled all four requirements.

The Nazis enshrined in their demonic laws that someone was a Jew if two out of their four grandparents were Jewish; one or both parents were Jewish or were enrolled as a member of the Jewish worshipping community. It is chilling to think that every ancestor of Jesus back to Abraham, if they had been alive at the time, would have been Jewish enough to qualify as a victim of the Nazi Nuremberg laws, and a victim of the Holocaust. Including, of course, Jesus the Jew.

## JESUS' CIRCUMCISION

Besides demonstrating the very real gendered humanity of Jesus, Jesus' circumcision shows that Jesus fully complied with the Mosaic Law.[*] The covenant of circumcision was Yahweh's 'Yes' to the sons of Abraham and the sons of Abraham's 'Yes' to Yahweh.

Self-consciously and proudly Jewish, the atheist journalist Howard Jacobson, in a *Guardian* column, titled 'Behold! The Jewish Jesus', observes: 'The last thing Jesus looks on the cross is Jewish', and he claims that Western artists have covered his naked privates not

---

[*] Luke 2:21.

out of modesty, but to avoid presenting Jesus as he would have been: physically circumcised, unequivocally Jewish.[36]

## JESUS AND THE JEWISH PASSOVER

The Nazi New Testament removed every reference to Jesus and the Passover – yet Passover is at the heart of Jesus' ministry and identity.

As the Mosaic law required of observant Jews, 'Every year Jesus' parents went to Jerusalem for the Festival of the Passover'. John's Gospel presents the ministry of Jesus within an *inclusio*: a literary bracketing by Passover. Jesus attended the Passover of his own accord three times: including at the start of his ministry and at the end.* Interestingly, John specifically titles it as the 'Jewish Passover'.

Paula Fredricksen, Professor of the Appreciation of Scripture at Boston University writes:

> What astonishes me when I read the stories about Jesus in the New Testament, is how completely embedded he is in this first century ... Jewish world of religious practice and piety. We tend to get distracted by the major plot line of the Gospels, because we're waiting for the story to develop up to the crucifixion. But, within that story, and the stories that are told by the evangelists that fills in the gap between the Galilee and Jerusalem, Jesus presented continuously as going into the synagogue on the Sabbath. He is presented as going up to Jerusalem for the pilgrimage holidays, specifically in John, for any number of pilgrimage holidays, and in the synoptic Gospels, most importantly, for Passover. Jerusalem at Passover is not the sort of place you'd want to be in unless you were really committed to doing an awful lot of ritual activity with tremendous historical resonance ...[37]

The Passover feast in Jerusalem frames the life of Jesus, vindicating his observant Jewishness; but more than that, this epic event commemorating the deliverance of Israel from Egypt by the

---

* Luke 2:41; John 2:13, 23; 6:4; 11:55; 12:1; 18:28, 39.

sacrificial blood of a lamb, when the angel of the Lord saw red and passed over, is the theological interpretative key to understanding his death. Jesus is the full and final prophetic fulfillment of all that this signifies, 'for Christ, our Passover lamb, has been sacrificed.'*

## JESUS' GENTILE TESTIMONY, 'KING OF THE JEWS'

This title is crucial for our Christology, particularly so as it is the testimony of Gentiles: ascribed to him by the wise men from the East and Roman soldiers from the West.

Just as the motif of Jesus and the Passover is an *inclusio*, framing the beginning and the close of his ministry, so also is the title 'King of the Jews', being referred to at the opening and closing of Matthew's Gospel, in the crib and on the cross. These literary frames must also frame our Christology.

*Jesus' birth title*: wise men from the East came to King Herod and asked, 'Where is the one who has been born king of the Jews? We saw his star when it rose and have come to worship him.'**

*Jesus' death plaque*: 'Above his head they placed the written charge against him: "This is Jesus, the king of the Jews". The religious rulers protested: 'Do not write "The King of the Jews", but that this man claimed to be king of the Jews.' Pilate answered, 'What I have written, I have written.'***

The Jewish leaders told Caesar's representative Pilate, 'Crucify him! ... We have no king but Caesar,'**** but now, Caesar's representative Pilate orders an inscription to be put up declaring Jesus as 'The King of the Jews'. It is written in Latin, Greek and Hebrew – for all the world to read and comprehend. We see in this both the particularity of Jesus' kingship (Jesus is King of the Jews) and the universality of

---

*   1 Corinthians 5:7.
**  Matthew 2:2.
*** Matthew 27:37; John 19:21–22.
**** John 19:15.

Jesus' kingship: in the languages of East to West – this Jewish King is the world's King. Some see in Pilate's plaque in universal languages a warning that crucifixion is what happens to anyone who claims to be king other than Caesar. But I suspect Pilate saw more than the Jewish authorities and this title is more than Pilate's pragmatism – it is public prophecy.

*King of the Jews?* How can the King of the Jews also be the King of the Gentiles? Here we must go back to the Biblical figure of Noah, the father of a new humanity after the flood. Noah gave the legal birthright of ruling his brothers to his second son, Shem; thus, Shem's legal heirs (*Shem-ites = Semites*) were divinely appointed to rule humanity. Abraham's father was a direct descendant of Shem – the inheritance and divine mandate passed to him and through that line to Abraham's second son Isaac, and from Isaac to his second son Jacob, whose name was changed to 'Israel'. The rightful King of Israel holds the long-handed-down baton of Noahic blessing to be king over all his brothers – all peoples.

Anti-Semitism has often made claims of a plot by Jewish bankers to rule the world – this old canard is intended to caricature and incite fear and hatred. However, could it be that in this lie that wicked men perpetrate, they pick up on the demonic fear of the Biblical fact that one day a Jewish man, a Jewish king, will indeed rule the world.

God became a Jew. And the church uncircumcised him.

Does all this Jewishness of Jesus really matter? Absolutely. Firstly, because to worship a non-Jewish Jesus is to worship a false God – it is blasphemy and idolatry. God is who he is in his self-disclosure. He gave himself to us as a Jewish man. Secondly, a Christianity divorced from Jewish roots is in danger of becoming a Gentile cult that Jesus and his Apostles would not recognize. Thirdly, because a

Christianity divorced from Jewish roots has *always* opened itself to a spirit of anti-Semitism and becomes complicit with the demonic.

Many portraits of Jesus do not look Jewish – Christian art added a loincloth to cover embarrassment of seeing God as a fully human, circumcised Jew. But interestingly, and significantly, the Jewish Belarussian painter, Marc Chagall, following the terrors of *Krystallnacht* in 1938, presented to the world a powerful portrait of Jesus the Jew titled 'The White Crucifixion'. Jesus is shown, not wearing the loincloth of Western art for modesty, but wearing a *Tallith*, the Jewish prayer shawl of an observant circumcised Orthodox Jew. The twentieth-century Hassidic Orthodox Jewish Chagall knew a first-century Orthodox Jewish Jesus.

Phyllis Stroh, an American Orthodox Jewess was out for a walk one day and saw a sign for a 'Hebrew-Christian Church'. She decided to go along, assuming it was an interfaith dialogue. To her surprise it was not, and instead she listened to a Jewish speaker claiming Jesus as Messiah. As he spoke, Phyllis had a vision of Jesus who spoke to her about himself as fulfilling numerous Old Testament passages and prophecies:

> Then I noticed, as this information was being poured into me, tears were streaming down my face, almost in torrents. I couldn't stop them, nor did I want to stop them, because it felt as if I were being washed inside, all over, everywhere, inside and outside. Indeed, I was being washed and cleansed, thoroughly and completely of all sin. I was born anew! Born again! I was given the fresh start I had longed for: *a new beginning*! The chance to start all over, with all the old stuff forgiven and washed away, was being given to me – as a gift, a miraculous gift! ... As I walked and wept, I thought, 'In one moment, if someone had put me on the rack and tortured me – I would never have believed in Jesus. But now, the next moment, I can do nothing but believe in Jesus, the One I had always been taught was a false, Gentile god.'[38]

# CHAPTER 5

# HE INVITES US TO HOLD HIM

*And he tenderly touched the leper*

*Simeon took him in his arms and praised God*
LUKE 2:28

In just the briefest of brush strokes, the Gospel writer Luke presents a breathtaking cameo of an encounter between the infant Jesus and the aged prophet. Luke doesn't tell us, but ancient sources suggest Simeon could be Simeon ben Hillel, head of Sanhedrin until 10AD, the son of famed Jewish Rabbi Hillel and father to the equally famed Gamaliel who taught Paul. Others think Simeon is the Simeon who was High Priest at the time of Jesus' birth. We cannot be certain, but what we do know is that Luke piles up godly predicates to describe this old priest and prophet: righteous, devout, waiting for God, anointed by the Spirit, attentive to the voice of God, living by faith in God's word.

In accordance with Mosaic Law, forty days after giving birth to a son, Mary brings herself and the infant Jesus to the temple to offer sacrifices, to present Jesus to God and to receive ritual purification. The ceremony turns into an epiphany as this elderly, godly man sees God's work and declares God's word.

## SIMEON HELD JESUS

Simeon took Jesus in his arms.* Simeon held in his arms the one who holds the whole world in his hands. God is not a shadow, a dream, a spectre, a doctrine – God is a person; God who is eternal spirit, is here in flesh and blood. It has never been enough for God merely to be known by us, to simply be believed in by us – to be talked to at a distance, to be affirmed in words and creeds. God has always wanted more. The goal of creation was always to hold and be held by God in a lovers' tryst in paradise. Jesus willed from all eternity to be brought to us and held by us – if not one way before the great fall, then another after the fall. And Jesus opened wide his arms from crib to cross, inviting embrace. He was held by his mother Mary – he was swaddled and cared for. He allowed a sinful woman to anoint his feet and kiss them; he blessed the woman with the issue of blood who held on to him, as the crowds pressed in on him. He allowed John to lean on his breast at their last meal together, and invited Thomas to put his finger into the wounds in his hands, his hand into his side. He allowed people to touch him, he comes to us, up close and personal, not distant and aloof.

While for a brief moment, at his resurrection, Jesus told Mary, 'Do not hold on to me, for I have not yet ascended to the Father' – because this was not the moment – and yet, even this statement shows that his disciples felt able to, would be inclined to, hold on to him. Then, when he had risen, he sent his Holy Spirit so that we might forever hold God, up close and personal.**

It is not God, but rather humankind that has made and kept a distance. The Old Testament prophet Isaiah mourned with God,

> No one calls on your name
> or strives to lay hold of you ...

ISAIAH 64:7

---

* Luke 2:28.
** Luke 7:44–46; Mark 5:25–34; John 13:23; John 20:27; John 20:17.

The church has long treasured this truth of holding Jesus. In the Anglican wedding service, bride and groom offer beautiful vows as each gives themselves to the other, beginning with the words 'to have and to hold, from this day forth'. That familiar phrase 'to have and to hold' actually originates from land conveyancing, where land was assigned to another: *habendum et tenendum*. Drawing on the concept of legal exchange, in the medieval meditations on the cross, *Charters of Christ*, Jesus' stretched out, crucified body is depicted metaphorically as a parchment paper, his blood the ink and his death a legal charter for us to inherit the kingdom. Here in his own blood Jesus writes:

> To havyn and heldyn that swete place [to have and hold in that sweet place]
> Wel gud in pes thourch my grace [well good through my grace] ...[39]

The reformer Martin Luther was fond of the theme of clinging to Christ. He voices Jesus saying,

> Whatever good thing you lack, look to me for it and seek it from me, and whenever you suffer misfortune and distress, crawl to me and cling to me. I, myself will give you what you need and help you out of every danger.[40]

The last recorded words of Katharina, Luther's wife, on her deathbed, on 20 December 1552, were 'I will cling to Christ like a burr to a coat'.[41] Ignatian spiritual exercises encourage us to apply our imagination to the holding of the infant Jesus – grasping something of his dependency, humanity, vulnerability and given intimacy. The Protestant and Puritan traditions speak of prayer and study of Scripture as the place where we take hold of God. The saintly Anglo-Catholic Edward Pusey wrote, 'Mary in her womb did hold Christ the natural body, the Priest holdeth the mystery of the body'[42] and understood that we who receive bread and wine, by faith and the agency of the Spirit, mystically and spiritually hold and are held by Jesus.

I remember the first time I held my now wife in my arms, in November 1987; the first time I held my newborn sons in my arms, in February 1998, and December 2001; and I remember the first time I held onto Jesus and was held by him, in June 1985. Maybe you have never held Jesus – perhaps kept an irreverent distance, or even a reverent distance – now, even as you read this, he invites you to come and hold. Maybe you once held him near and dear, but other things filled your heart and hands – like Simeon, take Jesus in your arms and hold him. Origen, the great early church theologian, wrote, 'For, as long as I did not hold Christ, as long as I did not embrace him in my arms, I was locked up and could not escape my chains.'[43] But this is true not only of Simeon, but of the whole human race. Anyone who departs from this world, anyone who is released from prison and the house of those in chains, to go forth and reign, should take Jesus in his hands. He should enfold him with his arms, and fully grasp him in his bosom. Then he will be able to go in joy where he longs to go …

## SIMEON BEHELD JESUS

*For my eyes have seen your salvation*
LUKE 2:30

Simeon is a name meaning 'hearing', from the Hebrew *shama*. Simeon hears God as he is seeing salvation history unfold before his eyes.

Like Job who spoke many centuries before, Simeon can say 'I have heard of you but now my eyes have seen you'. Simeon had been told by God's Spirit he would not see death until he had seen the Lord's Christ.* This same Spirit brought Simeon into the temple, and there he sees God in flesh brought into his temple. And Simeon

---

* Job 42:5; Luke 2:26.

hears and sees and knows and speaks, for here he is, just as God promised: the Messiah, Israel's king, the world's Saviour.

The one who holds, beholds. Seeing is believing. Most people in the temple saw just another young Jewish boy from an artisan family in northern Galilee – nothing special, not the only babe and mother in the temple that day. Only Simeon and the prophetess Anna had a spirit awake to God and eyes to see. How many others crowded the temple that day – there to offer sacrifices for sin, thank offerings, prayers, or just wanting to be near the holy place, near God – and failed to realize God was right here – if only they had eyes to see? The remarkable author and activist, Helen Keller, was blind and deaf from the age of two. She was once asked by a young boy, 'Isn't it the worst thing in the world to be blind?' Keller replied, 'Not half so bad as to have two good eyes and see nothing.'[44]

So many failed then to see who this Jesus was and so many today still are blind to him.

## SIMEON SAW SALVATION

'For my eyes have seen your salvation,
    which you have prepared in the sight of all nations'
LUKE 2:30–31

This child's name was a clue: Jesus, or *Jehoshua*, means deliverer, rescuer, saviour. But Simeon doesn't need a name to see a destiny. This child will grow up and save the world by not saving himself. This baby, offered to God at the presentation in the temple, will grow and present himself as an offering for sin – this held child will hold the world's sin to himself.

And who is this salvation for? Not simply Israel. But a salvation *prepared for all nations*; for we all need saving, for we all have sinned and fallen short of God's glory and we all face death and divine wrath. But those who hold and behold Jesus are saved and may depart in peace.

The medieval artist Rembrandt crafted two major paintings, and several drawings, of Jesus' presentation at the temple. It clearly captured his imagination over several decades of his career. The first depiction he painted when he was just starting out in Amsterdam, aged twenty-five. It is a traditional grand Dutch wide-angle scene, the artist's viewpoint set well back, observing the many observers, with great attention to the details of temple architecture and finely finished clothing. The young Rembrandt is showing his skill. Four decades later, the day after Rembrandt died, they found in his workshop a personal painting, a private painting – not a commissioned painting. Was it his last painting? Again, it is of Simeon and the presentation of Jesus. But so different from his youthful, detailed work. This is devoid of all externals, no architectural temple details, no people, no frippery and finery. The focus of the artist is on Simeon's old face, bathed in light as he is holding and beholding the luminous Jesus.

And Simeon's face is Rembrandt's own face. This is a self-portrait and his mouth is open, as he sings the *Nunc Dimittis*; his eyes half closed in awe, shielded from Jesus' light. No longer is Rembrandt a gifted young artist at a distance, detached and observing a scene, showing us all his skills of imagination and observation and representation; now he is an old man, like Simeon was, and he paints himself inside the story, and it is just him and Jesus, and now he is ready to have his Lord let his servant depart in peace, for Rembrandt's eyes have seen God's salvation.

The Victorian Oxford priest, John Keble, wrote:

> [Christ] is near at hand. You have but to lift up your eyes and look, and behold Jesus Christ visibly set forth, crucified among you. He is in His church, He is in His Scriptures, He is in your prayers, He is … in His Sacraments.[45]

Put yourself in the story – reach out, look up, to hold, and behold, Jesus.

# CHAPTER 6

# HE WALKS WITH US

*He took upon himself our very nature so he might give his nature to us*

*I will walk among you and be your God, and you will be my people.*
LEVITICUS 26:12

The British constitution has something known as the Order of Precedence. This lays out the hierarchy of the royal family and the position they take relative to each other at formal state events. The Queen, as head of state, must always walk at the front. The Duke of Edinburgh, as consort, walks behind her. The Prince of Wales as heir apparent ranks higher than the Duke of Edinburgh, but the Queen has formally issued royal letters patent that allow the Duke to come up higher at such formal functions, and walk one step behind her. The extraordinary privilege of the Christian faith is that the Son of God, the King of kings and Lord of lords has issued divine royal letters patent so we can walk *with* him – not merely process behind him, but with him, alongside him, next to him.

## IT HAS ALWAYS BEEN GOD'S DESIRE TO WALK WITH US

The Bible's big idea is not man walking with dinosaurs, but man walking with God. From the beginning, Adam and Eve 'heard the sound of the LORD God as he was walking in the garden in the cool of the day'.* In their sin they fled from God, and, fearing the worst,

---

* Genesis 3:8.

they hid in the shadows. But God didn't drive them away, push them away or even walk away himself; God walked to where they were. Adam and Eve, in their sin and self-willing, turned their backs on God, but God didn't turn his back on them; he came to them, walking in the cool of the day. And even when the consequence of their sin is expulsion from the paradise of Eden, God closed the gates behind him and walked them out, and the whole Bible story is God accompanying humanity through the corridors of history, directing them back to Eden.

Genesis, the first book of the Bible, the foundational book, proudly promotes this paradigm of walking with God. Enoch is a mysterious figure that we know next to nothing about, apart from the fact that twice it is said he 'walked with God'.* Noah, in an age of chaos, was righteous and is recorded as a man who 'walked with God'. When *Yahweh* meets the patriarch Abraham, he invites him, 'I am God Almighty, walk before me…' And Abraham did, and earned the title 'friend of God'.**

This theme of walking with God will define the relationship between God and Israel. In the law, God says, 'I will *walk* among you and be your God, and you will be my people.' Moses instructs Israel as they are about to enter the promised land to *walk* in his ways. Sadly, they often chose to reject this invitation and suffer the consequences of walking away. God beckoned Solomon to '*walk* before me faithfully with integrity of heart and uprightness, as David your father did', and he did for a while, before walking away. The prophet Micah reminded the people, 'what does the LORD require of you? … to *walk* humbly with your God'. In the (often tragic) histories of the kings of Israel and Judah, the writer frequently summarizes their lives by whether they walked in the way of God or whether they walked in the wicked way of their fathers.***

---

* Walking with God: Genesis 5:24; 6:9; 17:1.
** 'Friend of God': 2 Chronicles 20:7; James 2:23.
*** Leviticus 26:12; Deuteronomy 8:6; Micah 6:8; 2 Kings 21:22.

There is a beautiful song by the legendary Irish folk singer Mary Black called 'flesh and blood'. The chorus goes,

> Oh come on walk with me, talk with me,
> Tell me your stories
> I'll do my best to understand you
> You're flesh and blood, flesh and blood
> Don't refuse me your love …[46]

It has always been God's desire and design to walk with humankind.

## JESUS CAME WALKING

The incarnation of Jesus fleshed out God's plan to walk with us. God walking in our shoes. Jesus crossed time, space, eternity and divinity to walk with us. American astronaut, Jim Irwin, was one of only eight people to walk on the moon (at least, at the time of writing). He went to space agnostic, but he returned a passionate Christian, leaving NASA to start his own Christian mission. He stated:

> The entire space achievement is put in proper perspective when one realizes that God walking on the earth is more important than man walking on the moon. I believe that God walked on the earth 2,000 years ago in the person of Jesus Christ.[47]

From the Gospel accounts we read twice that Jesus rode a donkey, twice that he travelled by boat, and everywhere else that he walked. He walked from Galilee to Jerusalem; he walked the *Via Dolorosa* carrying his cross; he walked victorious out of the tomb of the dead; he walked to join the two mourners on the road to Emmaus and left them with burning hearts; he walked into the presence of his Father on our behalf, representing us, sitting down at the right hand. Jesus walked out to his disciples in their distress on the stormy sea. We often make much of the miracle of Jesus walking on water – treading chaos underfoot – but far more meaningful to me are Mark's words:

'Jesus came toward them, walking on the water.'*

I love the lyrics of the Blue Grass Gospel song: 'God walks the dark hills':

> The ways, the byways
> He walks through the billows
> Of life's troubled sea
> He walks through the cold dark night
> The shadows of midnight
> God walks the dark hills
> Just to guide you and me[48]

## JESUS WALKED TOWARDS US TO INVITE US TO WALK WITH HIM

Before his rise to stardom, the controversial artist Kanye West wrote a song titled simply 'Jesus Walks'. It was about how Jesus walks with all kinds of people and is told from the perspective of a drug dealer contemplating God. Kanye West played it to many music executives who all turned him down because it didn't conform to the accepted stereotypical form of rap. But Kanye knew Jesus walks with any and all, whatever side of life they come from. Kanye's mum, in her biography of her son, recalls one night when 300 teenagers gave their lives to Christ after an appeal when 'Jesus Walks' was performed.[49]

The tax collector was Israel's public enemy number one: a Jew who took money from his own people to pay their enemies, the Romans, and then made a profit on the side, adding on to the tax whatever he wanted, and even this was enforced by the Roman soldiers. A traitor. But Jesus is not choosy who his travelling companions are:

---

* Mark 6:48 (NLT).

*As he walked along, he saw Levi son of Alphaeus sitting at the tax collector's booth. 'Follow me,' Jesus told him, and Levi got up and followed him.*

MARK 2:14

# JESUS WALKS WITH US THROUGH DEATH TO LIFE

*Even though I walk through the valley of the shadow of death,*
*    I will fear no evil,*
*for you are with me;*
*        your rod and your staff,*
*        they comfort me.*

PSALM 23:4 (ESV)

## JESUS WALKS TOWARDS US AND WANTS TO WALK WITH US

The earliest Christians were not called 'Christians', but 'people of the Way', those who walked the way of the cross with Jesus. They were pilgrims, sojourners, travellers, walkers with God. There is an oft repeated meme that challenges us to 'walk as Jesus walked', and that is true: so we should, as we read in 1 John 2:6. But that imperative is preceded by 'whoever says he abides in him'.* Walking as Jesus walked is a sign of abiding in him; we can't walk like him unless we first come close. Abraham and Isaac are both said to have walked *'before* God' – a translation from the Hebrew word *paniym*, literally, 'face'.**

It could easily be translated as they 'walked looking at God's face'. Let us walk *consciously* as Paul says, 'fixing our eyes on Jesus'; and as the writer to the Hebrews encourages us, 'looking to Jesus'.*** To

---

* 1 John 2:6 (ESV).
** Genesis 17:1–12.
*** 2 Corinthians 4:18; Hebrews 12:2.

walk conscious of Jesus means we must take our eyes off ourselves and look on him to lead. To walk conscious of Jesus means we go in the same direction that he sets and at his pace. That may prove costly. To walk conscious of Jesus may mean we may be led where we don't want to go.

To walk with Jesus will require constant confession of our sin as our proximity to divinity exposes the shadows and cobwebs in our lives.

Nothing trips up walking with God like sin – and we all sin. One main Hebrew word used for sin is *het*, which means, literally, to 'go astray'. The Greek or New Testament understanding of sin is of wrong thinking, but the Hebrew idiom conveys more of a sense of taking a wrong path, certainly a recognition that we have strayed, about faced, stopped. When we repent, when we turn away from wrong and turn toward God, God forgives, meets us on the path and walks forward with us.

We are to walk in constant *communication* – we must talk as we walk. Jesus speaks – he talks to us mainly through his word recorded in the Bible. Here the speaking God speaks to us and directs our steps – this ancient word is now a word for us, a lamp to our feet and a light to our path. And as we walk, we talk to Jesus – EM Bounds, the noted writer on intimacy with God, said 'we walk with God down the avenue of prayer'.[50]

I have not often found that prayer comes easily. I am quickly distracted. I find I can fall asleep in any position praying, but walking helps me be attentive. One discipline that has helped me has been my wife Tiffany driving and dropping me off miles from our home to allow me to walk back, and for a couple of hours, imagining the Lord beside me, we would walk and talk.

I learned this many years ago, when a door seemed to close for Tiffany and me on our plans for the next step in ministry. I took time off work and walked across the Mendip hills, seeking God for advice and for the next step. And then he spoke to me. He told me to go to Trinity College and study theology. I was appalled. Already in full time ministry, having planted a church and now helping lead it, I thought college and theology an unnecessary abstraction. Knowing that I was protesting out of pride, the Lord spoke to my inner ear loud and clear: 'You are arrogant to think you cannot learn from what I have told my people in the past.' I accepted a place at theological college and for the last thirty years have followed the doors that the Lord opened because of that God talk on a God walk.

The saintly Methodist leader John Fletcher of Madeley is said to have prayed at all times, regularly spending all night in prayer, and when walking, greeting his friends he would ask the question, 'Do I meet you praying?'[51] It is said the first sign of madness is talking to yourself – I suspect many might think I'm going mad for I always walk and talk to the Lord. But then I often see people walking along the road, headphones in their ears, talking – I presume they're on their phone. Why not put your headphones in, put some music on and walk and talk out loud to the Lord – cultivating a constant communication with Jesus.

## YOU WERE MADE TO WALK WITH GOD

Your feet were made for walking. If we believe the evolutionary scientists, for seven million years, humanoids have been walking. James Levine, professor of medicine at the famous Mayo Clinic College said, 'Humans were designed to walk.'[52] Apparently, the amount of time we now spend sitting down is having an adverse effect on our physical health and contributes towards many diseases, otherwise preventable. Hippocrates, the father of modern medicine, said 'walking is the best medicine' and that advice still holds true millennia later – the NHS devote a whole web page to 'walking for health'. Walking is the best medicine for our bodies and walking with God is the best medicine for our souls. I like the Danish philosopher Kierkegaard's advice to his sister, Jette, in 1847:

above all, do not lose your desire to walk. Every day, I walk myself into a state of well-being ... But by sitting still ... the closer one comes to feeling ill. Thus if one just keeps on walking, everything will be all right.[53]

We were made to walk with God, and when we don't, we get sick. One of the saddest verses in the Bible says, 'many of his disciples turned back and no longer followed him'. Jesus never walked away from anyone – but many walked away from Jesus – and into the shadows. When we meet the two disciples on the road to Emmaus we read, 'they stood still, their faces downcast', but after walking with Jesus they were transformed, saying, 'Were not our hearts burning within us?'* Walking with Jesus transforms situations, he transforms emotions, he transforms lives.

I have been corresponding with someone who grew up in an abusive Christian context and who had walked away from religion. But three decades later, as she revisited her formative experiences, she found God had not given up on her. She wrote to me,

'My closest sense of God now – and a very warm and loving one, as well as often intensely joyful – comes when I take long walks alone across the countryside, usually several times a week. Then I might not see another human for three or four hours and I do feel as though I have a presence who walks beside me. There is a great beauty and peace in that.'

Indeed, there is. She had walked away from institutional religion; God had not walked away from her. On the contrary, God pursues her and still wants to walk with her. And when God comes 'beside' her, she experiences his graces, as she describes her feelings: 'warm, loved, joy, beauty, peace'. Some might protest it's just exercise endorphins, wind on her face, or the wonder of creation – but this woman knows: the divine joins her walking. And she loves it.

---

* John 6.66; Luke 24:17, 32.

This is a well-documented experience as recounted in the many remarkable stories in John Geiger's *The Third Man Factor*. The title owes something to the poem by TS Eliot and draws from the experience of the explorer Shackleton in the Antarctic, when on a perilous journey over ice mountains he and his colleague were aware of a strange accompanying presence:

> Who is the third who walks always beside you? When I count, there are only you and I together. But when I look ahead up the white road, there is always another one walking beside you.[54]

There is always another walking beside you – the Lord, inviting you: 'walk with me'. Jesus walked along the Galilee shoreline and called people to him. Jesus walked to the disciples on the stormy sea and dispelled their lurking fears. Jesus walked to the mourners on the Emmaus Road and turned and set their hearts on fire.

Jesus walks alongside you and says, 'Walk with me'.

# CHAPTER 7

# HE IS THE WATER OF LIFE

*He overflowed in restless love and created humans in his image to love*

> *'So – this – is – a – River!'*
> *'THE River,' corrected the Rat.*
> *'And you really live by the river? What a jolly life!'*
> *'By it and with it and on it and in it,' said the Rat. 'It's brother and sister to me, and aunts, and company, and food and drink, and (naturally) washing. It's my world, and I don't want any other. What it hasn't got is not worth having, and what it doesn't know is not worth knowing. Lord! the times we've had together!'*[55]

That classic work of English philosophy, *Wind in the Willows*, makes the point so well. The River. We need to live by it and with it and on it and in it. The river of God frames life with God. Followers of Jesus are river people. The Bible places human life at the head of four rivers in the Garden of Eden and the Bible closes with life at the river in Paradise. The people of Israel enter the Promised Land crossing the river Jordan and Jesus begins his ministry of promise baptized for us in the river. The psalmist celebrated this river of God declaring, 'There is a river whose streams make glad the city of God'. In the prophet Ezekiel's remarkable vision we see a river flowing from beside the altar of God, flowing out from the temple to transform the marshes and desert, bringing life to land and sea, bringing industry, economy and vitality.*

---

\* Genesis 2:10–14; Revelation 22:1; Joshua 3:14–17; Matthew 3:13–17; Psalm 46:4; Ezekiel 47.

What is Ezekiel's river? Some consider it a literal river, from a literal temple in the millennial reign. Most interpret it figuratively, however. The church father Ambrose said that the river symbolizes the Holy Spirit; the Puritan John Owen said the river represents the mission of the church preaching the Gospel. The river is the royal graces of God – God's goodness outgoing, as the kingdom advances through the Gospel, by his Spirit. American novelist Mark Helprin wrote beautifully that 'A good river is nature's life work in song'[56] – God's river is God's lifelong work to sing over us in love and to bring life.

## JESUS BRINGS US THE RIVER

In John's Gospel we read of an extraordinary encounter between Jesus and a Samaritan woman at a well. As she draws up water from the well, Jesus asks her for a drink. She is somewhat taken aback: 'How is it that you, a Jew, ask for a drink from me, a woman of Samaria?'[*] That Jesus even spoke to her was shocking in that culture, to her, and to Jesus' own disciples who, on returning, 'marvelled that he was talking with a woman'.[**] Why the shock? Yes, she was a Samaritan, and Jews generally despised them for being Jews who had intermarried with Israel's pagan neighbours. But Jesus is not racist. Yes, she was a woman, and culturally in an ancient Semitic culture, men did not speak to women who were not their wives. But Jesus is not sexist. She was of a morally colourful past, having had several husbands and now living with a man not her husband. But Jesus is not moralist. She engaged Jesus in theology, something no woman would usually do with a rabbi , far less one she perceived to be a prophet. Jesus is not intellectualist, but desiring to engage and reveal the truth to all. Jesus asks for a drink, and when she responds, stunned, he says,

[*] John 4:9 (ESV).
[**] John 4:27 (ESV).

*'If you knew the gift of God, and who it is that is saying to you, 'Give me a drink,' you would have asked him, and he would have given you living water.'*

JOHN 4:10 (ESV)

When she expresses her confusion Jesus states:

*'Everyone who drinks of this water will be thirsty again, but whoever drinks of the water that I will give him will never be thirsty again. The water that I will give him will become in him a spring of water welling up to eternal life.'*

JOHN 4:13–14 (ESV)

Jesus knew that this woman had been thirsty all her life – she had tried satiating it by repeated relations with men – she had had five husbands – five! But there was only one man who could satisfy the deep longing of her soul, and that man was Jesus. There is a river whose streams make glad the city of God, and that river is given by Jesus to all who ask.

Thoreau said most people 'lead lives of quiet desperation'[57] – indeed, that describes the slow expiration, that longing and scratching around for that river that will satisfy. And all the while this life is there, waiting for us, offered to us by Jesus.

The very first story about human origins, in the Bible, makes much sense of this. It describes how we were made by God, like God, for God. Our first ancestors enjoyed deep connection with God, walking in the cool of the day with him, in the garden paradise of Eden. But our free will asserted itself against God and we ended up exiled, expelled from the garden, divorced from God – and now we all live east of Eden. Ever since then, there is, sown in the human soul, a sense of exile, of estrangement, a longing for home – we are not what we should be, and not where we should be.

JRR Tolkien put it this way,

> We all long for Eden and we are constantly glimpsing it; our whole nature at its best and least corrupted, its gentlest and most human, is still soaked with a sense of exile.[58]

So tragic, and yet so true for so many. Like this woman at the well, desperate to drink deeply of life. Jesus sees and Jesus satisfies.

Jesus made a similar promise sometime later[*] when he goes up to Jerusalem to celebrate *Sukkot*, the Feast of Booths (or Feast of Tabernacles). This proved to be a powerfully prophetic backdrop for Jesus to make a public revelation. On each of the seven days of the feast, a priest would draw water from the Pool of Siloam in a golden flagon and bring it in procession to the temple amid the joyful crowds and the sound of trumpets that always herald God's voice and victory. At the temple the water was poured into a bowl that fed through a tube to the base of the altar. This symbolic act was both a thanksgiving to God for the provision of water and a petition for rain the following year. Some rabbis and the Jerusalem *Talmud* understood this act to be prophetic of the anticipated messianic age and God pouring out of his Holy Spirit.

John tells us that on the last and greatest day of the feast – as the priest pours out the water that runs to the altar, the crowds joyful, expectant, watching, hoping, praying – at exactly that pregnant moment, Jesus stands up in the midst and commandeers the event and directs it to himself:

> 'Let anyone who is thirsty come to me and drink. Whoever believes in me, as Scripture has said, rivers of living water will flow from within them.' By this he meant the Spirit, whom those who believed in him were later to receive.

JOHN 7:37B–39A

[*] John 7:37–38.

The response was electric – some thought, rightly 'this is the Messiah!' others that this was a madman or blasphemer and wanted to arrest him. But no one dared.

Jesus was making a clear statement: he was the Messiah, he was Israel's Anointed, he was the one who could bring the Spirit, he alone could satisfy. The prophecies of God are focused on him; the promises of God are fulfilled in him. Jesus would bring the river of God; Jesus, the sacrifice for sin on the altar of Golgotha, from whose pierced side flowed blood and water, yes physical evidence of death, but holding a deeper spiritual significance – a river of blood to cleanse us from sin and a river of Spirit bringing life to the full.

## LOSING THE RIVER

The favourite psalm of the German Reformer, Martin Luther, was Psalm 46. The main focus for him was the understanding of God as a safe fortress, and based on this psalm Luther would write, '*Ein feste Burg ist unser Gott*' – A mighty fortress is our God' – which would become the battle cry of the Reformation. It is claimed that whenever Luther was depressed, he would say 'Come, let us sing Psalm 46', and history records that he sang it as he went into his trial at the Diet of Worms, not knowing if he would walk out alive.

I was once invited to preach at a conference near the beautiful city of Ulm, which is surrounded by hills and beside the mighty Danube. In one session I decided to speak on Psalm 46, on the river of God. Before the session, I gave the translator the theme and passage I would speak on. During the worship the translator rushed up to me all flustered. 'There's no river in Luther's Bible translation' he exclaimed, 'I've checked, it's not here'. Indeed. The version of Luther this pastor was using had edited out the river of God. Instead Luther had just 'brunnlein', little wells. I was shocked – how could the great architect of the Protestant Reformation, one of first translators of the whole Bible into the vernacular, omit to translate this verse?

Returning to Oxford I consulted Professor Lyndal Roper, a world expert on Luther. She helpfully dug into this for me and discovered that in Luther's early Psalter of 1524 Luther had *Strom* – German for 'river, tide, flow, current' – but strangely by his 1531 version, the translation had been altered, removing all trace of *Strom* – all we have is little wells or springs.[59]

I suspect this omission reflected the hardening of his theology that became more about fortress and less about flow. You cannot live the Christian life when God is a mighty fortress but not also a river whose streams make glad the city of God. Sadly, many try to. For many the gushing river of God has become a well. The woman at the well needed to drink from the river of God Jesus offered her. Luther left the river for the well.

## THE DEVIL LOVES A DESERT

In the classic French film *Jean de Florette*, a city slicker inherits a farm. When he arrives, he seeks to make a go of the farm and works hard, day and night, expending all his energy, efforts and savings investing in the latest agricultural techniques to make his farm viable. But despite his painstaking, back-breaking efforts, the blazing summer sun and the severe summer drought cause his crops to wither, his chickens begin to die and his artesian well dries up. Each day he wakes before dawn, and agonizingly crosses the mountain into the next valley with his donkey laden down with pots and pans and churns, to collect water from another running stream. But the little he can carry is never enough and soon everything dies. Eventually, in desperation, he turns to water divining and, thinking he has found an underground stream, he places explosives to unearth it. Tragically, a falling rock in the explosion strikes his head and he is mortally wounded. On his deathbed Jean admits, 'I failed to see that water was the one problem.'

The tragedy of this dark story is that all along there was a strong river running under his land, but it had been stopped up by wicked neighbours, who planned his downfall in order to drive him back to the city and rob him of his inheritance.

Water is the one problem.

Biologically, it is the necessity of all life, and spiritually, the Water of Life, the river of God, the Spirit of God, is the necessity of fullness of life. The devil wants to block up the river so that the world lives and dies parched. We scrabble around in our own effort trying to make a go of it, whilst all along the river of God waits to be found and to flow to us and through us.

## A FISH IN TROUBLE

Some years ago, we were holidaying in Normandy during one record-breakingly hot August. The heat actually melted the battery in my camera and damaged it irreparably. One morning, as I spent time praying, I sensed the Lord say he was going to reveal something important to me that day. I wrote this in my journal and went into the day expectant at what the Lord was going to teach me. It was a good day, spent at the sublime Mont Saint Michel. But nothing stood out as a word from the Lord. Back at the gîte in the late afternoon, I lay on my bed reflecting on the day and wondering where I had met the Lord and where I may have missed him. Had I been wrong with my sense, in what I'd written in my journal, that the Lord was going to give me a revelation? Meanwhile, Tiffany and my boys went to feed the giant koi carp fish in the large pond at the bottom of the garden.

Suddenly Tiffany's voice interrupted my thoughts, 'Simon, come quick, there's a fish in trouble!' I got up and rushed to the end of the garden and there, stranded in the mud, in a few inches of water, was a massive orange, black and silver carp, gasping for breath, fighting for life. Why it had swum into the shallow end I don't know; perhaps it had followed some tasty morsel, or perhaps this was a favourite spot in the cool of the day. Whatever the reason, the heatwave and the low water table resulted in drying up the pond to half its usual depth and this noble fish, beached in the shallows, was dying. Trying to wriggle back towards deeper water, this fish only embedded itself in the mud, it was stuck, gills part submerged, for a slow death. Tiffany and my boys stood appalled at this pathetic sight.

I told the boys to quickly bring a dustbin lid and a watering can, both of which we had used and were by the gîte back door. They ran off and quickly returned with them. Joel poured water on the fish, offering it momentary relief, and I stepped into the muddy pond, gently put both my hands under the huge but listless fish, and lifted it onto the dustbin lid. Joel constantly watering it, I carried it on the lid to the deeper end of the pond, where I lowered it back into the water. On the bank, Tiffany and the boys held their breath. The fish lay in the water momentarily motionless, and then suddenly it lunged to life and with a swipe of its tail and a swaggering flash of orange, black and grey, it turned and swam for the deep end. I climbed out, a hero, my family cheering.

Immediately as we headed back to the cottage, the Lord spoke to me.

'The church is like that carp: mature, distinguished, and impressive. But she has left the deep waters. And she is stuck in the mud and slowly suffocating. Momentary relief from the odd spiritual watering can of a renewal conference cannot save her. Her only hope is to get back to deep water.'

This was the revelation the Lord had told me in the morning he was going to give me. The church is out of the deep and in the shallows – the river has become a pond and the pond a puddle. And she is straining to breathe, fighting for life.

That evening my multi-coloured carp was seen leaping in the deep end – but his fellow yellow koi had not learnt from the near disaster. And so it was gutting on successive days to see other giant carp, though not my instantly recognizable giant orange and black friend, having made the same mistake but, with no help to hand, lying dead in the shallows. How many have never entered the river of God and are slowly dying of dehydration. And how many Christians, having once drunk deep draughts of the river of life flowing by the Spirit from Christ, have stopped drinking and now are gasping for life. Jesus says,

> 'Let anyone who is thirsty come to me and drink ... whoever drinks of the water that I will give him will never be thirsty again. The water that I will give him will become in him a spring of water welling up to eternal life.'

JOHN 7:37 AND 4:13–14

Let us finish with this challenge and invitation by the famed Baptist preacher, CH Spurgeon:

> 'Ask God to make you all that the Spirit of God can make you, not only a satisfied believer who has drunk for himself, but a useful believer who overflows the neighbourhood with blessing ... (seeing visitors in church) what a blessing it would be if they went back to their respective churches overflowing; for there are numbers of churches that need flooding; they are dry as a barn-floor, and little dew ever falls on them. Oh that they might be flooded! What a wonderful thing a flood is! ... Oh for a flood of grace! The Lord send to all our churches a great springtide! ... So may it be! ... may all of you who hear me this day get your share of the streams. Oh, that the Lord may now fill you and send you home bearing a flood of grace with you.'[60]

# CHAPTER 8

# HE IS WORTH IT

*And he loved the rich young ruler who loved his money more than God*
*And he turned over the tables in the temple to stop the money-changers ripping off the poor*

*Costly grace is the treasure hidden in the field; for the sake of it a man will gladly go and sell all that he has. It is the pearl of great price to buy which the merchant will sell all his goods. It is the kingly rule of Christ, for whose sake a man will pluck out the eye which causes him to stumble, it is the call of Jesus Christ at which the disciple leaves his nets and follows him.*

DIETRICH BONHOEFFER

The *Financial Times* headline read: 'Lost and found: Buried treasure is poised to reach a much wider audience'. The article was about a new exhibition of the so-called Cheapside Hoard – over 500 jewels found by builders working on an Elizabethan house in London in 1914. Included in the haul was a 400-year-old pocket watch set in a giant Colombian green emerald! The *Antiques Roadshow* jewellery expert said its value was 'truly priceless'. What a find! No wonder people flocked to the exhibition – fascinated by the dream that had become a reality for someone, the dream of finding buried treasure.[61]

An entrepreneurial business, picking up on this same dream, invites wealthy Americans and Canadians to pay £1500 to visit muddy fields in Britain with metal detectors, hunting for treasure – commenting that finding a 200-year-old coin is thrilling for those from relatively 'young' countries.* Everyone loves a treasure hunt. Every year, more and more people are taking up metal detecting for treasure; in 2017, some 78,000 archaeological items were unearthed across the United Kingdom and reported, with 1267 of these being declared 'treasure' by the authorities. The county of Norfolk produced the most finds, followed by Lincolnshire and Suffolk.

Jesus picks up on this same dream and fascination in a parable he told, about kingdom 'treasure'. He said, 'The kingdom of heaven is like treasure hidden in a field.'**

It was customary in the ancient world to bury treasure. Banks are modern repositories of people's wealth. In the medieval era wealthy folk bought impregnable strong boxes, treasure chests. In Europe, the Germans excelled in making the best chests with the most intricate keys and unpickable locks. Even today some don't trust the banks – I had a good friend who put all his money into gold sovereigns which he hid stitched into the lining of a coat. He trusted only one person with the knowledge of the whereabouts of the gold, but sadly when he died the chap's possessions were quickly disposed of by the next of kin who were ignorant of the sovereigns. Someone one day, buying an old coat on a market stall or charity shop will have a nice surprise. But the ancients kept their wealth in gold and silver coins and in jewellery and buried it in the ground. The Jewish Qumran Scrolls, dating from a century before Jesus, refer to treasure being hidden during the Roman occupation.

Many of us have daydreamed about finding treasure. In Irish folklore, leprechauns guard pots of gold at the end of the rainbow; the ancient Greeks and Romans had griffins guarding treasures; and

---

* Albeit all these relatively 'modern' countries, have their own ancient first peoples.
** Matthew 13:44.

who doesn't thrill to the story of *Treasure Island* or *The Hobbit* with Bilbo Baggins finding the *arkenstone* amidst dragon Smaug's stolen treasure, or finding the Ring under the Misty Mountains.

Jesus picks up on this almost universal fascination with treasure, and he uses it as a metaphor to describe the kingdom of heaven. He is saying that the state where he, the Lord Jesus, is King, the state where his rule is sovereign – is treasure, and it is there for the finding, now. Jesus himself, life with him, in his way, under his influence, his loving rule and his presence, is the greatest possible treasure.

The Anglo-saxons addressed God as the 'High Treasure Keeper' in prayer. As indeed he is – but he isn't *just* the treasure keeper, he is more than that. He is the treasure *giver*.

The Greek word for treasure is *thesaurus* – a compendium of goodies. Treasure is something we find, something that we didn't earn or buy, something that we didn't make or merit or receive as a gift, but something that is rare and of value – otherwise it would be just rusty tat and mud. And treasure is life changing. One of the most significant recent finds was in Pembrokeshire, the discovery of an Iron Age chariot, dating from about AD25, and judging from the beautiful fittings which had been preserved, must have belonged to a high-ranking nobleman. It was bought by the National Museum of Wales for a considerable sum. The fortunate finder, Mike Smith said,

> 'I still can't believe it. Obviously I've read other people's finds. I've watched them on telly, and I've always thought, I wouldn't mind finding that, it's still surreal, and life changing.'[62]

Exactly. Life changing is the word. Jesus brings a kingdom that is treasure: something we didn't deserve, couldn't afford and is utterly life transforming. What is that treasure? It is God himself, it is the King, and when we receive the King, he comes with his kingdom, wherein is forgiveness, fullness of life – eternal life.

Now, we all know that where there's treasure there are often pirates who would steal it and bury it. In Jesus' parable the man who discovered the treasure 'quickly covered it' lest someone see and steal his find. The devil is a pirate who would steal and hide the treasure. He tells us that God has no treasure for us. He makes us look in the wrong place or go after 'fools' gold'. The Apocalypse of John depicted the enemy as a dragon – and we all know dragons love to steal and sleep on a bed of treasure.

Daniel wrote that Nebuchadnezzar, the Babylonian King, besieged Jerusalem, stole the treasure from God's house and placed it in the treasury of his own god.[*] Sometimes it is not satanic deception or theft, it's just the warp and weft of life that causes us to lose the treasure that was once ours. Maybe, reading this, you know there was a time when you savoured the Saviour Jesus and enjoyed his privileges, but somehow life's exigencies caused you to lose that treasure. Like the woman in the parable of the lost coin, light a lamp, sweep the house, search carefully and rejoice at finding what you have lost.[**]

A Polish lady once told me that she remembers Germans coming to her home when she was a child. She lived near the German border in an area that had been populated by Germans in the Second World War. The elderly Germans came with family members and merely wanted to revisit old memories, in their former house, which they had to abandon in haste and flee west as the Russian soldiers advanced in 1944. The Polish lady told me that this was quite common in her area, and there were many stories of visiting Germans coming to find treasure or valuables they had hidden in the house walls, or under the floors, which they could not access in their haste to flee danger. Maybe as you read this you might recall something of the treasure the Lord has given you, but that got left behind. Come back and claim it.

[*] Daniel 1:2.
[**] Luke 15:8–10.

## THE PLEASURE OF HIS KINGDOM

*'The kingdom of heaven is like treasure hidden in a field, which a man found and covered up. Then in his joy he goes and sells all that he has and buys that field.'*

MATTHEW 13:44 (ESV)

Jesus speaks of the man's great pleasure, his great joy at his find. The Greek word is *eureka*, which conveys immediate joy. Joy is the emotion of the kingdom – joy is the fruit of the Spirit, joy is the overflow of those who find Jesus. When the angels announced Jesus' birth, they declared 'joy to the world' – to truly meet Jesus, to receive his gifts, is to know joy unspeakable and full of glory.

Life is full of hard knocks for most and no one sails through it without stormy seas. For many, life is spent more like Eeyore than in awe, as if we have mistaken hemorrhoid cream for toothpaste.

The medieval mastermind, Thomas Aquinas, once wrote

'man cannot live without joy – therefore when he is deprived of true spiritual joys, it is necessary that he become addicted to carnal pleasures.'[63]

Indeed, and these momentary reliefs never fully satisfy. St Thomas was already an established theological Doctor of the Church with numerous publications that would dominate Western thought for centuries – philosophy, poetry, a massive series of systematic theology. At the end of his life, it is said the Lord spoke to Aquinas, 'Thomas, what do you want?' And he replied: '*Non nisi te Domine*' – 'Nothing but you, Lord'. You see, to have Jesus is to have the treasure beyond compare.

In the seventeenth century, Blaise Pascal was the genius of his age – mathematician, philosopher, inventor (of the first mechanical calculator), his intellectual contributions are still studied and celebrated today. When he died, a piece of parchment was discovered sewn into the breast of his doublet, over his heart. It was his treasure – not gold sovereigns, but a golden experience from which he would never recover.

He had had an encounter with God so profound that the words describing it tumble out like babbling bubbling lovers' language, not the precise prose of a philosopher and mathematician.

> Year of grace 1654, Monday 23 November, feast of St. Clement ... from about half past ten at night to about half an hour after midnight, FIRE. God of Abraham, God of Isaac, God of Jacob, not of philosophers and scholars. Certitude, heartfelt joy, peace. God of Jesus Christ. God of Jesus Christ. 'My God and your God.' ... Joy, Joy, Joy, tears of joy ... Jesus Christ. Jesus Christ. May I never be separated from him.[64]

Now that is a treasure!

CS Lewis wrote of his conversion to Christ, going up Headington Hill on a bus, when, after months of debate and struggle he committed and submitted to Jesus. He did so as a rational decision, because he believed the evidence that Jesus was the Son of God and Saviour of the world. He records that he wasn't expecting to be 'surprised by joy.'[65] Joy sneaked up on him. The treasure is Jesus himself but when we find him, we find joy. Later Lewis wrote that 'Joy is the serious business of heaven.'[66]

The celebrated preacher, John Piper, writes how, in 1968, Pascal and CS Lewis, among others, and the Bible 'teamed up to change my life forever with those words, "Joy, Joy, Joy, tears of joy."' Piper records his encounter with Pascal's epiphany:

> I always feared that it was sin. That wanting to be happy was a moral defect. That self-denial meant renouncing joy, not renouncing lesser joys for greater joys. But then God conspired with these writers to force me to reread the Bible. To give it a chance to have its true say. And what I found there concerning joy changed me forever. I have been trying to understand it and live it and teach it ever since. It's

not new. It's been there for thousands of years.[67]

Listen, God has placed treasure for you to find, it is the Gospel, his kingdom with all its pleasures, his Son who gave his life, a king's ransom, paid to bring you home. Find God and start enjoying God.

## THE MEASURE OF HIS KINGDOM

*'in his joy, he goes and sells all he has and buys that field'*

MATTHEW 13:44B

Finally, Jesus tells us there is a measure for this kingdom, a price and a cost. The Greek emphasizes the cost. There is an extra word in the original that is rather lost in translation *panta hosa* (which sounds a bit like a Mexican tapas bar) literally: he sells *all* (*panta*) *as much* (*hosa*) as he has. The finder of the field with the treasure has a choice to make: to continue with his life as it is and forget or forfeit the field of treasure, or to give *all* he has to gain the field of treasure. There can be no holding back just in case – no partial exchange – it's all or nothing – and the treasure finder is all in. A new start in life, a new life to start, means selling up the old life. There are many people only too ready to give up everything to gain something better. One man set up a website called *All My Life For Sale* and sold off everything he possessed, 600 items, including a set of false teeth, personal photos and his winter coat. Ashley Revell, when 32, sold everything he owned, raised £70,000, went to Las Vegas and bet the lot in one throw on a roulette wheel. And won. Returned with £140,000 and started up an online poker game – which later went bust.

The kingdom of heaven, however, is not a game of risk, not a gamble – it is an exchange for a treasure we have already discovered is real. The kingdom of heaven cannot be had on the cheap – it will cost you all you have and all you are. The kingdom of heaven is not an additional field on your existing field. The kingdom of heaven is not a hobby. You cannot go on living the way you lived once the treasure that is Jesus comes into your life. You are confronted with a challenge, a decision, it is either/or not both/and. When one treasure seeker found what he was looking for, he asked Jesus 'what must I do to inherit eternal life?' and Jesus looked lovingly at this rich young ruler, and said, 'go, sell all that you have and give to the poor, and you will have treasure in heaven; and come, follow me.'*

Jesus was not implying that we've got to buy this treasure in heaven, buy the life with him that is offered. No, you could never afford it. But the treasure hunter must sell what he has to buy the field, must give all he has to receive God's gift, must make room for it. This is the paradox – the kingdom of heaven is free but it's not cheap. The kingdom won't take more than you've got, but it will take all you've got. Jesus said, 'where your treasure is, there your heart will be also.'** The rich young ruler was not prepared to give all for Jesus, for eternal life – we are told he went away 'very sad' – with savings but not saved. A very poor rich man.

Not so the treasure finder in the parable, who sold his possessions and bought the field and claimed the treasure, joyfully.

Dietrich Bonhoeffer, the church statesman martyred by the Nazis for opposing Hitler in the name of Christ, coined the term 'cheap grace' to describe Christians who want something for nothing. In his book *The Cost of Discipleship* he writes:

> Costly grace is the treasure hidden in the field; for the sake of it a man will gladly go and sell all that he has. It is the pearl of great price to buy which the merchant will sell all his goods. It is the kingly rule of Christ, for whose sake a man will pluck out the eye which causes him to stumble, it is the call of Jesus Christ at which the disciple leaves his nets and follows him.[68]

Jesus sings over us, he offers himself, his love, his kingdom, his

---

* Mark 10:17, 21 (ESV).
** Matthew 6:21.

glory, his eternal life to us. Jesus himself, life with him, in his way, under his influence, his loving rule and his presence, is the greatest possible treasure we could ever find, and for this priceless offer of treasure he simply asks we give ourselves to him.

The treasure, the pleasure and the measure of his kingdom. These rhymes might seem a little contrived, but they help me remember that the greatest marvel of Christianity is not actually that God offers all this, but *why* would he, *why* does he? The simple answer that we will never fathom; because *we* are God's treasure, *we* are God's pleasure, and Jesus' death is the extreme measure God pays to have us.

# CHAPTER 9

# HE WAS A MOUNTAIN MAN

*And he was transfigured and revealed in all his glory*

*After six days Jesus took Peter, James and John with him and led them up a high mountain, where they were all alone. There he was transfigured before them.*

MARK 9:2

My portly girth belies the fact I was once a bit of a mountain man – while acknowledging that old men call hills or fells 'mountains'. In our twenties and thirties, Tiffany and I spent time in the mountains at every opportunity, mainly the Lake District, but also Scotland, the Brecon Beacons, the Swiss and French Alps. I have had some memorable mountain top experiences. On Helvellyn, at Christmas, I sat in the snow and fed a mouse that joined me for lunch. On Ben Nevis I tore a ligament in my knee, and the three-hour ascent became a five-hour descent, as I was half carried down by Tiffany. On Scafell I got to the top huffing and puffing, only to see a 6-year-old girl in a loud pink onesie and pink wellies, skipping about and as fresh as a daisy. In the Swiss Alps, God told me clearly to not pursue an academic theological path that was before me, and to go and get ordained.

In the Bible there are several significant mountain top experiences:

- The Garden of Eden was on the mountain of God (Ezekiel 28:13–14)
- Noah's Ark came to rest on Mount Ararat, as flood waters receded (Genesis 8:4)

79

- Abraham offered Isaac on Mount Moriah – and God provided the sacrifice (Genesis 22)
- Moses met God on Mount Sinai, and received the Ten Commandments (Exodus 19 – 34)
- David built the City of Jerusalem on Mount Zion (2 Samuel 5:7)
- Solomon built the Temple of God on Mount Moriah (2 Chronicles 3:1)
- Elijah confronted and destroyed Baal's false Prophets on Mount Carmel (1 Kings 18)
- Jesus gave his most famous sermon 'on the mount' (Matthew 5 – 7)
- Jesus was arrested on the Mount of Olives (Matthew 26:30)
- Jesus was crucified on the mountain of Golgotha (Matthew 27:33)
- Jesus ascended from the Mount of Olives (Acts 1:9–12)

In the Bible mountains matter – they are places of significant spiritual experience. The artist and poet William Blake once wrote, 'Great things are done when men and mountains meet'.[69] This is true, and even more extraordinary things happen when men and mountains and God meet.

## ON A MOUNTAIN HIGH, HE WAS TRANSFIGURED
### HE CONFRONTS EVIL ON ITS OWN GROUND

*After six days Jesus took Peter, James and John with him and led them up a high mountain, where they were all alone. There he was transfigured before them.*

MARK 9:2

Jesus led Peter, James and John up a *horos hupselos*, a 'mountain high'. The third century Church Father Origen suggested this particular mountain was Mount Tabor, a prominent hill in Galilee, and this subsequently became a popular pilgrimage place, and the site of the Church of the Transfiguration. However, Mount Tabor is almost certainly wrongly identified, being in the wrong place for the setting of this Gospel account. The previous story offered by Mark is set at Caesarea Philippi, a town which is at the base of Mount Hermon. At the time of Jesus, Mount Tabor was a Roman fortress and inhabited and so hardly a place for quiet retreat and dramatic divine revelation for the disciples. And Mount Tabor is not really a 'mountain high', but more a big hill at 575m. The 'mountain high' of the transfiguration is almost certainly Mount Hermon. Situated in northern Galilee, which is now on the Lebanese/Syrian border, it is Israel's highest peak at 2800 metres high.

In Hebrew, *hermon* means 'sacred', from the root HRM and related to a modern Arabic word *haram*, which means 'forbidden'. Hermon was certainly a sacred mountain in Jewish culture, though mainly associated with pagan worship. Archaeologists have discovered over twenty pagan shrines on its slope, caves with pagan carvings to Baal, the storm god who always sought to steal the affections of the Hebrews. This mountain was a centre for Baal worship, literally a 'High Place' for pagan excesses mixing the demonic, erotic and naturalistic. Ancient Ugaritic texts say Hermon was where Baal the storm god had his palace on earth.

Ancient Jewish myths claimed it was the gateway for the wicked fallen angels who produced the Nephilim, the race of giants who were believed to have lived there. The late fourth century translator of the Bible into Latin, St Jerome, rendered Hermon in his translation as 'anathema'.

So, Jesus brings his disciples here, to Hermon, to the haunt of demons, to an occult high place, that stood in total defiance of the God of Israel. Six days before, in Caesarea Philippi, Jesus chose the Roman temple to the god Pan, whose giant cave mouth was nicknamed 'the Gates of Hell', to make a significant declaration. It was here that he declared himself to be God's Messiah and boasted that he would build his church and the gates of hell would not prevail against him. A powerful public prophetic challenge and a declaration to the demonic. And now, days later, he makes the same gesture on another demonic site, only this time it is God and the great Old Testament figures who declare who he is before all the hordes of hell. The calculated irony of it! Jesus chooses Satan's turf, the gateway for evil spirits, the lair of wicked giants, the mountain saturated in demon shrines, he chooses here to show who is Lord. On this place that existed to humiliate Israel and challenge her God, Jesus stands and humbles Hell.

What is Jesus like? He is like one who is unafraid to confront the most feared and greatest evil on its own doorstep.

## HE REVEALED HIS TRUE NATURE

*and he was transfigured before them*

MARK 9:2B

Generally mountains humble humans: they are ancient, vast, immovable, intimidating. Here was Israel's most magnificent mountain, yet, this figure climbing it caused the mountain to tremble. The word transfigured is *metamorphoo*, from which we get our English word 'metamorphosis', meaning to change form, experience transformation, be changed-through. Jesus didn't change form, but unveiled something of his nature, his true being, hitherto unseen. Jesus is simply unveiled, revealed, disclosed as he is in blazing divinity. This was not Jesus showing off, just Jesus showing himself.

In our culture, literature has always loved the motif of ordinary people with extraordinary powers who are more than they appear:

Strider the Ranger who is Aragorn the king;[70] Clark Kent the journalist who is Superman; Bruce Banner the scientist, who is the Incredible Hulk. These ideas are as old as the Greek heroes Perseus, Achilles, Odysseus and the wonder woman Hippolyta. These are all myths, figments of human imagination. But not so Jesus. The carpenter from Nazareth is the High King of Heaven. God incognito is now on display in his divinity, deity, majesty, glory.

I love how the remarkable Holocaust survivor, Viktor Frankl, expresses worship, 'The angels are lost in perpetual contemplation of infinite glory.'[71] Peter, James and John have a glimpse of what angels see – infinite glory. It must have sucked the breath out of them. This vision expanded their view of Jesus. They have been with Jesus and seen Jesus for two and a half years – Jesus the teacher, the prophet, the woodworker, the wonder worker. They have seen him weary and asleep on a boat and also magnificently striding across the waves. They have seen him engage and hold the mesmerized crowds and tenderly blessing the children. They have seen him all the rage and causing outrage. But they have never seen him like this – as he was, as he is, glorious. O how we need to have our vision of Jesus expanded and see him as he is.

## HE WAS BLAZING WHITE

> ... and his clothes became radiant, intensely white, as no one on earth could bleach them

MARK 9:3

That sounds a little like an advert for household bleach – 'white & shine' or 'whiter than white' – but the Gospel writer is simply straining to find words to describe the utterly exceptional and ineffable.

Hermon is sometimes known by the Arabs as the 'snowy mountain' because it is covered in snow for a third of the year –

which melts in spring and feeds the Sea of Galilee. Did Jesus take them up when there was snow on the ground? Was this a picture of Jesus blazing white, so intensely pure, that he made the pure snow look grubby?

## HE KEPT COMPANY WITH THE CHAMPIONS OF HEAVEN

*And there appeared before them Elijah and Moses, who were talking with Jesus.*

MARK 9:4

The pagans believed this mountain was a 'thin place'. Here heaven and earth kissed. And we suddenly see appear those who passed from this earth into eternity eight hundred and thirteen hundred years earlier, step into time and speak with, encourage and honour Jesus. Here, Moses represents the Law as giver, as writer of Israel's Torah. Elijah represents the Prophets – in many respects pre-eminent among them, it is Elijah who the Scriptures anticipate returning to prepare the way for the coming of God's king on earth. Here he is.

The ancient Greek storyteller Aesop coined the phrase 'A man is known by the company he keeps' – well, Israel's two greatest figures, greatest men of God, champions of heaven, are here to honour Jesus – to make much of him.

What is Jesus like? He is like the greatest of all who ever walked on earth.

## HE WAS AFFIRMED BY GOD HIMSELF

*And a cloud overshadowed them, and a voice came out of the cloud, 'This is my beloved Son; listen to him.'*

MARK 9:7

It's one thing to have Moses and Elijah as your proposer and seconder

– quite another to have God. The cloud is a familiar Biblical motif: it speaks of God imminent but transcendent. God came down to Israel in a cloud; God led Israel through the wilderness in a cloud; most importantly the cloud descended on the Ark in the temple, God presencing himself with Israel. Sadly, after the repeated sin of Judah, the Babylonians invaded, and the ark was lost. And worst of all, the cloud of God's presence was gone – *ichabod*, the glory has departed. Jewish hope and belief was that when the Messiah came, God's cloud of glory would return. And here it is – here God is, here the king is. And the voice of God speaks, just as it spoke in the beginning, and the voice said, '*This is my beloved son*'. The Father says ,'that's my boy'. God's eternal Son, God's beloved Son. The disciples have often heard Jesus speak of God as 'my father' but now the disciples hear the Father say 'my son'. Just days before Jesus asked them 'who do men say that I am, who do you say that I am?' – now, on the mountain, God answers the question.

## THE MOUNTAIN WHERE JESUS WAS TRANSFIXED

No sooner has the cloud of God lifted, and the two witnesses departed, than Jesus turns and heads back down the mountain. Peter has suggested that he could perhaps build a booth, a shelter and prolong this experience. But there's work to do, and down in the valley is a demonized boy who needs setting free. And there's another mountain to climb, a hundred miles south, where in just a few months the climax of the ages will be staged.

> *And as they were coming down the mountain, he charged them to tell no one what they had seen, until the Son of Man had risen from the dead. So they kept the matter to themselves, questioning what this rising from the dead might mean.*

MARK 9:9–10

This theme he would expound in days to come:

*The Son of Man is going to be delivered into the hands of men, and they will kill him. And when he is killed, after three days he will rise.*

MARK 9:31

In Tolkien's *Lord of the Rings*, the travellers have been refreshed and encouraged in the splendour of Rivendell. But time is pressing, evil is rising, and they can delay no longer. Elrond, ruler of the kingdom of Elves says: 'The Ring-Bearer is setting out on the Quest of Mount Doom. On him alone is any charge laid.' On the Mount of Transfiguration Jesus has been in council with his Father, witnessed by Elijah and Moses, but now Jesus must set out on the quest, the charge on him alone is laid – he is heading for his mount doom. This meeting on the mountain was not just an epiphany for his disciples. It was not just to reveal the eternal glory, majesty and divinity of Jesus. It was to prepare Jesus for what was ahead. To steady and steel him. It was here that Jesus is tempered, and so, resolved, he strides down this mountain towards the next, to meet his nemesis in holy battle. Reinhold Messner, unquestionably the world's greatest mountaineer – the first man to ascend Everest without oxygen, and the first to ascend all fourteen of the world's 8000 metre peaks said, 'Mountains are dangerous'. His own brother died in a tragic accident – Jesus walked to a death that would be no accident.

From the Mount of Transfiguration Jesus makes his way to the Mount of *Transfixation*. On Mount Hermon Jesus is 'seen through' but soon on Mount Golgotha Jesus will be 'pierced through'. On the Mountain of Transfiguration Jesus is declared the Son of God – but Jesus descends and describes himself as the Son of Man, and on that other Mount of Transfixation, as representative humanity, he will die for the sins of whole world. Here God came down in a cloud, but there darkness will descend and Jesus will cry from God-forsakenness. Here two of Israel's most venerated men are his witnesses; there, two of Israel's notorious criminals. Here clothed in white, there the sins of the world laid on his nakedness. Here, they shielded themselves from his blazing glory, there they will turn away in horror.

Only God could pay for the great sins of humankind. Only man should pay for the sins of humankind. So Jesus, the Son of God, becomes the Son of Man, and as the representative man, wears our sin and shame, and bears the punishment for the sins of the world. In our place, in our stead, as our substitute, he dies for us – and in so doing, presents us with his glory and his divine sonship. And incredulously, these disciples who are in awe today, who have seen great and wonderful things, who have heard the Father's testimony of Jesus, these very men will deny him and abandon him who will see it through to the bitter end – transfixed, pierced through and held to Golgotha's Gibbet by rough hammered nails, twisted pain, and substitutionary love.

Jesus' mountain top experience is for our mountain top experience. Jesus is transfigured, then Jesus is transfixed, so we can be transfigured. When we put our faith in Jesus – when we look to him in faith, the Son of God glorious, and the Son of Man at the cross nefarious, we who are by sin disfigured are by grace transfigured, robed in divine glory, and the Father calls us his beloved sons.

- Calvary is our Mount Eden where God walks with us in paradise.
- Calvary is our Mount Ararat where God's judgment ceases.
- Calvary is our Mount Moriah where God provides the sacrifice of his son.
- Calvary is our Mount Horeb where God calls and commissions us.
- Calvary is our Mount Sinai where God reveals his eternal law.
- Calvary is our Mount Carmel where God destroys the works of the evil one.

- Calvary is our Mount Zion where Messiah establishes his glorious reign.

CS Lewis wrote,

> The sweetest thing in all my life has been the longing – to reach the mountain, to find the place where all the beauty came from ... All my life the God of the mountain has been wooing me.[72]

Come to the mountain of God, and meet with him, and know that beauty, and find longing fulfilled.

# CHAPTER 10

# HE IS ROYAL

*And he showed us he was the king of the kingdom*
*And he showed us that his was a kind kingdom*

> *Rejoice greatly, Daughter Zion!*
> *Shout, Daughter Jerusalem!*
> *See, your king comes to you,*
> *righteous and victorious,*
> *lowly and riding on a donkey,*
> *on a colt, the foal of a donkey.*
> ZECHARIAH 9:9

In his fascinating book, *Like Jesus: Shattering our False Images of the Real Christ*, Jamie Snyder describes a 'Jesus Doll' – a 'huggable, washable and talking Jesus plush doll' who 'comes sporting fuzzy dreadlocks and a satiny beard'[73] billed by manufacturers as a 'wholesome alternative to teddy bears'. When you pull the cord it says '*I love you*,' '*I have great plans for your life,*' and '*be good to your mother and father.*' If you were to design a huggable, talking Jesus doll, what phrases would you choose to describe him? Many of our images of Jesus are indeed false, and they do need shattering.

Distinguished New Testament Professor Thomas Schreiner argues that one of the unifying themes for the Bible is God's kingdom, whose goal is to see the King in his beauty and be enraptured in his glory. Amen. Jesus came and proclaimed the kingdom of God and declared himself as the King. Whatever different images we have of Jesus, the picture of King must be front and centre.

England has had some unforgettable kings. Edward the Confessor, the so-called 'crowned monk' who built Westminster Abbey after taking back England from the Danes. Richard Lionheart, a warrior king who led the third crusade to regain Jerusalem for Christendom. Henry III who was devoted to piety, prayer and the conversion of the Jewish people. Henry VIII, as wide as he was tall, with nice legs in stockings, six wives, no heir and a power struggle with Rome that still rumbles on. James I, who united England and Scotland; the nations flourished under his reign and he commissioned the famous authorized King James Bible. Charles I, who some call the *Martyr*, beheaded as a traitor for bringing civil war and hiring mercenaries against his own people. Charles II who restored the monarchy, and reigned over an era that became a byword for hedonism, libertinism and cynicism. George III, nicknamed the Mad King, who was known for his eccentricities and extremes. Undoubtedly some of Britain's best kings have been queens: the Celtic Boudicca, a warrior queen who fearlessly fought the occupying Romans. Elizabeth I who defeated the greatest Empire of her day, the Spanish, and made Britain Great. Victoria, on whose Empire the sun never set, stretching as it did from East to West. Our own much-loved Elizabeth II who has served over a crumbling Empire with grace, faithfulness and integrity.

In John's Apocalypse, Jesus, the conqueror of evil and ruler of heaven and earth, is given the title 'King of kings'.[*] This title had been claimed by Persian kings over a millennium before Jesus, but the Hebrews reserved it exclusively for Yahweh – *HaMelachim Malchei*. It's one thing to claim a name like the Persian rulers, quite another to own the name. And he who sits enthroned in heaven, ruling the universe, wears it by right.

---

[*] Revelation 19:16.

## JESUS' KINGSHIP IS RACIAL

There is a racial line, a specificity to Jesus' kingdom and kingship: he is the King of the Jews, he is David's seed and Lord, he is the King of Israel, he is King of Zion, he is the one of whom the psalmist prophesied: 'I have installed my king on Zion, my holy mountain.'* Jesus' ancestry through his stepfather Joseph descends from succession to the rightful King on David's throne – he was a legitimate heir to the throne, in contrast to the line of Herod, who were appointed by the Romans. At his birth, the wise men from the East came to Herod and said 'We have come to worship him born king of the Jews'. Pilate asked Jesus, 'Are you the king of the Jews?' Jesus didn't deny this but expanded its scope. On his death plaque, the words 'king of the Jews' were written in the main languages of the world, for all to understand: Latin, Greek and Semitic – he is King of kings. It is to and through the Jewish King, that God's kingdom is revealed and given to the world.**

Just as Queen Victoria was an Englishwoman ruling her vast Empire – so a Jewish King sits enthroned in heaven and rules the universe. I have often wondered if the ancient and universal hatred of Jews is not really a projection of a deep rejection of the King of the Jews – Jesus. The spirit of anti-Semitism is the spirit of the anti-Christ, that ancient serpent who forgot his place and sought to sit in Christ's place, and exalt his seat above God's throne. Few Jews today recognize their Jewish King – Israel is a secular state ruled by a democratic government. But one day all that will change – all Israel will be saved, and all Israel ruled by their Jewish King.

* Psalm 2:6.
** Matthew 2:2; Luke 23:3; Matthew 27:37.

## JESUS' KINGSHIP IS UNIVERSAL

The prophet Zechariah calls him the 'king over the whole earth', while Timothy and St John give his heavenly title as 'King of kings'.*

Though there is a particular locus and focus of Jesus' kingship of the Jews, he is not a parochial king, whose rule is restricted between Jordan and the Mediterranean. Jesus is not one king among many, he is King of all kings, King over all time, all peoples, of all creation – there is no sphere outside the stretch of Jesus' royal sceptre. In my church, St Aldates, we have a stained-glass window, and the focus is a variation of one of the most famous images of Christ, Christ stood over the world, which sits like a ball at his nail-pierced feet. Christ *Pantocrator* – the ruler of all. We do not yet see all things under his feet** but the final outcome is not in question – it is just a matter of time. One day he will return, and then, at his nail-pierced feet every knee will bow, and every tongue confess that he is Lord.

The mid-twentieth century German New Testament professor, Oscar Cullmann, employed an analogy to explain the now and not yet of the rule of Christ and his kingdom. In the Second World War there were two defining days, D-Day and VE Day. On D-Day, the Allied forces landed in Normandy and spearheaded the retreat of the German forces all the way to Berlin. The D-Day landing was decisive in determining the end of Hitler's regime. There would be much fierce fighting in the days ahead – but victory now was never in doubt. Twelve months later VE Day was declared, full unconditional surrender of the Germans. Analogously, the first coming of Jesus was the inauguration of God's kingdom, a D-Day, the decisive beachhead to retake the world from the grip of the demonic. The second coming of Jesus and the full consummation of God's glorious kingdom is like VE Day, total victory – and Jesus will sit enthroned and judge the living and the dead, finally destroying all sin, death,

---

* Zechariah 14:9; 1 Timothy 6:15; Revelation 19:16.
** Hebrews 2:8.

disease and the demonic. We live during the in-between ages, the kingdom is now and not yet – there is work to be done, battles to be fought, but the kingdom advances inexorably.

## CHRIST'S KINGSHIP IS HUMBLE

Zechariah prophesied his coming:

> *Rejoice greatly, Daughter Zion!*
> *Shout, Daughter Jerusalem!*
> *See, your king comes to you,*
> *righteous and victorious,*
> *lowly and riding on a donkey,*
> *on a colt, the foal of a donkey.*

ZECHARIAH 9:9

Alexander the Great is said to have entered India in a grand procession of two hundred painted war elephants, two hundred painted camels, two hundred soldiers riding black horses backwards, then in the golden throne hoisted on an ivory chariot sat Alexander – followed by two hundred tame lions: and heralds marching and proclaiming: 'I am the Lord of the universe. I conquered the world. Now I will conquer the stars.' Wow, what a display, magnificent, decadent, there would have been no mistaking just how great Alexander thought himself to be, as conqueror of the nations. But, one day, he will join all others, at the same level, at the feet of Jesus and throw his crown down and acknowledge the one who conquered death.

Many men aspire to be God, some are considered by others as God. But only Jesus is the man who *is* God. Who ever heard before of a God who became man? Yet the Son of God left unapproachable light and stepped into the darkness and was steeped in darkness to bring us to light. The eternal king chose a stable for a nursery and the cross for a throne.

There are various legends and fables of ancient kings 'disguising' themselves as one of their poor subjects and walking amongst them. This trope is seen in Shakespeare, Kierkegaard and Tolkien, among others. There's even a comic book series called 'kings in disguise'. But Jesus is not a king in disguise, he is not merely *pretending* to be meek. Saint Paul writes of the remarkable incarnation:

> *who, being in very nature God,*
>> *did not consider equality with God something to be used to his*
> *own advantage;*
> *rather, he made himself nothing*
>> *by taking the very nature of a servant,*
>> *being made in human likeness.*
> *And being found in appearance as a man,*
>> *he humbled himself*
>> *by becoming obedient to death –*
>>> *even death on a cross!*

PHILIPPIANS 2:6–8

Because he has walked in our shoes, lived in our skin, he knows of what we are made – remembers we are but dust – as the Puritan Richard Sibbes wrote:

> He shed tears for those that shed his blood, and now he makes intercession in heaven for weak Christians … He is a meek king; he will admit mourners into his presence, a king of poor and afflicted persons. As he has beams of majesty, so he has a heart of mercy and compassion.[74]

No wonder Mark in his Gospel records 'the common people heard him gladly.'*

---

* Mark 12:37 (NKJV).

## CHRIST'S KINGSHIP IS POWERFUL

There are twenty-one European Royal families living in exile. There are a couple of dozen more royal families who are recognized as monarchs in their country but have no executive power to govern. Of all the European royal houses, only Liechtenstein (population 36,000) has any actual executive authority involved in government. Jesus is not a mere figurehead monarch. Jesus holds a sceptre – he is King of a kingdom – he rules with divine executive power from his throne. There is an ancient concept of a *dualism*, in which equal and opposite forces are held in creative tension, underpinning the ordering of the universe: good and evil, spirit and matter, light and dark, or Yin and Yang. We see it in Eastern Zoroastrianism, Chinese Taoism, Greek Gnosticism, and in Mueller Light Yoghurt. Jesus' power needs no antithesis to define itself. There is no isometric demonic equal and opposite force. Jesus' kingly power may, for a time, be contested, but it is never compromised.

Isaiah spoke of that arrogant ancient serpent Satan seeking to rise above the throne of God – but he was hurled down to the pit.* Satan arraigned his kingdom armies against Christ's, but it was never a fair fight. He always fights dirty, and Jesus always triumphs.

How does Jesus rule in power? The Greek father of political philosophy, Plato, wrote:

> There will be no end to the troubles of states or indeed of humanity itself, until … political power and philosophy [wisdom] thus come into the same hands …[75]

I wonder if Paul knew this quote, and if he was referring to it directly when he spoke of 'Christ the power of God and the wisdom of God'.** In the movie *Gladiator*, Emperor Marcus Aurelius says to his daughter Lucilla, 'If only you had been born a man, what a Caesar

---

* Isaiah 14:13.
** 1 Corinthians 1:24.

you would have made.' Then he adds, 'You would have been strong. I wonder, would you have been just?'[76]

Jesus was and is and will be – ruling with power, and wisdom and love and justice.

## CHRIST'S KINGSHIP IS ETERNAL

*Now to the King eternal, immortal, invisible, the only God, be honour and glory for ever and ever.*

1 TIMOTHY 1:17

There is a notion that kings are immortal because they live on in their heir seated on their throne, hence the proclamation, 'The king is dead, long live the king.' Some ancient kings aspiring to divinity strove for immortality. They built monuments and tombs to themselves to live on in memory. Just think of the great pyramids, mausoleums for the Pharaohs, hoping to be propelled into divinity. The Roman Empire lasted 500 years. The Muslim Caliphate lasted 800 years. The British Empire lasted 250 years. The Soviet Union lasted 70 years. The Ottoman Empire lasted 700 years, remarkably and suddenly collapsing 5 weeks after the Balfour Promise was made and handed to those who made it. Hitler promised a thousand-year Reich, a satanic millennium, which crumbled in insanity and infamy.

To Jesus belongs the kingdom, the power and glory, for ever and ever. Jesus has no fixed term of office, there are no presidential or prime-ministerial elections, he has no successors, no rivals, no equals, there is no contest. Jesus was King before time and will be King when time has run its race.

Only a living king can rule – so the demonic powers at Calvary wanted to hear 'The king is dead!' and seized their opportunity when Jesus assumed human flesh. The incarnation made the immortal Son of God vulnerable – God-in-flesh could die. Satan sought to kill Jesus at his birth, when King Herod ordered the slaying of the innocents; at the start of his ministry, when Satan tempted him: 'throw yourself off the temple, and ultimately in Jerusalem, when Roman soldiers nailed him to a cross. But Satan signed his own death warrant in Jesus' blood. Even the terrors of torture and death could not tarnish his crown. That cruel cross he turned into a throne, his death into life. In the words of Shakespeare's Richard II, 'Not all the water in the rough rude sea can wash the balm off from an anointed king.'[77] Only a living king can rule and only a king who treads down death can rule forever. The morning prayer in Jewish office, prayed daily by devout Jews states 'The Lord is king, the Lord was king, the Lord will reign forever more'.

So how do we respond to this King of kings? The first and last reference to kings in the Bible both reflect worship given to King Jesus. The first is when the enigmatic Melchizedek meets Abraham returning with bounty from war. He is King of Salem, whose name would later have the suffix added and become Jeru-salem. His name, Melchizedek, in Hebrew means 'my king (*melek*) is righteous (*tsedek*)'. This king of righteousness is the King of Salem, that is the King of peace. The psalmist said 'righteousness and peace kiss each other'* and they do in this mysterious man. And he brings a gift of bread and wine to nourish the war-weary Abraham. And Abraham, the lesser, honours the greater, and worships him and gives him a tenth of all the plunder.** Who is Melchizedek? Is this a pre-incarnate Jesus? A Christophany? At the very least he is a prefiguring. The writer to the Hebrews says, Jesus is the forever Melchizedek:

- Jesus is 'a priest *forever* in the order of Melchizedek' (Hebrews 5:6)
- Jesus is a 'high priest *forever,* in the order of Melchizedek' (Hebrews 6:20)

*   Psalm 85:10.
**   Genesis 14:18.

- 'without beginning of days or end of life … he remains a priest *forever*.' (Hebrews 7:3)
- Jesus is 'a priest *forever*' (Hebrews 7:17)
- Jesus is 'a priest *forever*' (Hebrews 7:21)
- Jesus 'has a permanent priesthood' (Hebrews 7:24)
- Jesus 'is able, once and *forever*, to save those who come to God through him' (Hebrews 7:25, NLT)
- Jesus 'lives *forever* to intercede with God on their behalf' (Hebrews 7:25, NLT)
- God 'appointed his Son with an oath, and his Son has been made the perfect High Priest *forever*' (Hebrews 7:28 NLT).\*

Abraham worshipped Melchizedek with a tithe, and we worship Jesus with all we have – he is greater, he is worthy, he is the King of peace, he is King of righteousness, he is King of Jerusalem, and he meets us and graces us with bread and wine.

The final reference to kings in the Bible is at the very end, and here all the kings of the earth come to the City of God, and 'bring their splendour into it' – to Jesus they pay homage, the King of kings.\*\* According to the Rabbis, in Midrash commentary, the first words Adam uttered in Eden were – *Adonai malakh olam va'ed*: 'The LORD is King for ever and ever'. That is the last word too, the everlasting word. To adapt Egyptian King Farouk's line:

> In the end there will only be five kings – the four in a pack of cards, and Jesus.[78]

# CHAPTER 11

# HE IS THE WAY

*And he opened the way to God for us*

*'I am the way and the truth and the life.*
*No one comes to the Father except through me.'*
JOHN 14:6

A few years ago, I had the privilege of preaching the Good Friday and Easter Sunday Sunrise services for Easter pilgrims at the Garden Tomb in Jerusalem, one of the claimed sites for Jesus' crucifixion and burial, and certainly in the right vicinity. It was one of my life's greatest privileges. I arrived a few days early, and stayed in accommodation at the Garden Tomb, giving my time to prayer and preparation. Each day some 2000 people came on pilgrimage, to worship and pray and thank God at this site set apart to remember. What struck me was the sheer diversity of those who came – Indonesian, Nigerian, American, Scandinavian, Indian, Mongolian – most groups wearing their own distinct cultural tribal clothing, and all praying, praising and celebrating communion in their own language, united by Jesus. It was unforgettable, a foretaste of heaven.

What is it about this Jesus, a humble carpenter from Galilee two thousand years ago, that summons the affection and devotion of millions around the world, crossing centuries, cultures, languages, ages – all united in loving Jesus? I was struck by how many wept openly, overwhelmed. What is it about this Jesus that commands such love, such allegiance? What do these people know, what have they experienced?

## SEE HOW JESUS CARES

*'Do not let your hearts be troubled.'*

JOHN 14:1

The disciples were troubled. Could it be just a week since they had accompanied Jesus triumphantly into Jerusalem – the air pulsating with joy, the crowds lining the streets and pressing in to be near the Messiah – the celebrating and the shouting and the hosannas, and the hope that at last a king had arisen who would drive out the defiling Romans, and put things right? And then the extraordinary events in the temple. The miracles, and the confrontations with the authorities, and the taking control by overturning the tables of the money changers and driving out the vendors. But now it seems Jesus hasn't followed through with their plan – if anything he's pulled back. And people are shaking their heads at him and some are whispering in the corners; and Judas has been acting furtively and even Jesus has not been himself, withdrawn, his mind elsewhere. There is a strange spirit abroad – it is sucking the air from their lungs – this night their senses are alert, adrenalin is surging, everyone is on edge, suspicious, anxious.

In the film adaptation of Tolkien's trilogy, *The Fellowship of the Ring,* the hobbits have made it to the Prancing Pony and are enjoying some supper when Strider (Aragorn) joins them.

> 'Are you frightened?' he asks Frodo.
> 'Yes' replies Frodo.
> 'Not nearly frightened enough, I know what hunts you.'[79]

Well, darkness is abroad, and it is Jesus who is being hunted here, and the disciples sense it. Jesus knows only too well this will be their Last Supper. Within a few hours he will be betrayed, rejected, falsely accused, tried, beaten and mocked, tried again, tortured and executed. In a few hours, he will enter fully into our fallen humanity and bear the sins of the world on his shoulders. And his Father, entwined in love from forever, will turn away from him, and all alone he will be harrowed by hell. And yet Jesus, despite the storm clouds gathering, in remarkable selfless grace seeks to comfort them. It is they who should be comforting him, within hours they will come for him. But see how he cares. And he seeks to allay their fears, saying, 'do not let your hearts be troubled'.*

Fyodor Dostoevsky once wrote,

> I believe there is no one lovelier, deeper, more sympathetic, more rational and more perfect than the Saviour; I say to myself with jealous love that not only is there no one else like Him, but that there could be no one.'[80]

Surely he was never lovelier than on this night, at supper with his friends, gracing them, as the demonic spun its web. *Forbes Magazine* carried an article which stated, 'No one cares about you.'[81] It suggested many of us are stifled by fear of man and we need to get over ourselves, because we don't matter, no one actually cares about us. The worst thing I have ever had to do as a priest is to conduct the funerals of those who commit suicide. I have sat at several hospital beds with others who have unsuccessfully attempted to end their lives. Why do they do this? There are many reasons, but there is a shared experience, and sadly the often very false perception among those with suicidal idealism that nobody cares for them, that they are all alone, and that their situation has no hope of improving.

That perception is of course a deception. There is someone who cares, and who understands, and wants to be with you and can transform the situation. He always has, and always will. His name is Jesus.

That night when hell was moving in on the Prince of Heaven, Jesus cared. And he would face all that would come his way that night precisely because he cared for them and for you and for all.

---

* John 14:1.

Years after this Last Supper, one who was there, and scared, could write 'cast all your anxiety on him because he cares for you'.[*]

Jesus never promised us a trouble-free life. On the contrary he shortly tells his disciples, 'in this world you will have trouble'.[**] Trouble is unavoidable and following Jesus invites more. But trouble will not be the song they sing in their hearts. No, they will not let their hearts be troubled even if their situation is troubled – there is peace to be found even in the storm. How can they transcend these troubles – Jesus says: *Don't be troubled – trust in God, trust also in me.* The answer to troubled hearts is to trust in God, who is there. See how he cares.

## AND SEE WHAT JESUS SHARES

*'Trust in God, and trust also in me.'*
JOHN 14:1 (NLT)

The Greek word that is translated trust here is *pisteuete* and it means to have faith, belief, trust, to entrust. Encouraging them to 'trust in God' would sound like a reasonable thing for them to be encouraged to do, but remarkably Jesus adds to that 'and also trust in me'. A doctor might say 'trust me', and maybe we do, or maybe we don't. A politician might say 'trust me.' But this is more than that. Here Jesus says, 'trust in me' and places himself as equal with God as the object for their faith. Jesus is to be afforded the same commitment as God: *You believe in God, believe also in me; you trust in God, trust also in me; you entrust yourself to God, entrust yourself to me.* A few sentences later[***] Jesus uses an unusual personal pronoun, *ego eimi* = I, I AM. This is the very title God reveals as his personal name in Exodus 3 to Moses (*Yahweh* – I am who I am) which is rendered in

[*] 1 Peter 5:7.
[**] John 16:33.
[***] John 14:6.

the Greek translation of the Old Testament, the Septuagint, as *ego eimi*. John, who leant against Jesus at the final supper, is writing his Gospel and conveying what Jesus did and said on that fateful night – when Jesus declares his divinity and prepares for his death.

But what do we make of this extraordinary claim, to name himself as God? This is not the saying of a rabbi, or a philosopher or religious leader or prophet. Plato, Socrates, Buddha, Mohammed never made such bold claims, blasphemous claims, unless true. Generally people who claim such things are in psychiatric institutions. Now, what are we to make of this? CS Lewis gets to the heart of it:

> I am trying here to prevent anyone saying the really foolish thing that people often say about Him: I'm ready to accept Jesus as a great moral teacher, but I don't accept his claim to be God. That is the one thing we must not say. A man who was merely a man and said the sort of things Jesus said would not be a great moral teacher. He would either be a lunatic – on the level with the man who says he is a poached egg – or else he would be the Devil of Hell. You must make your choice. Either this man was, and is, the Son of God, or else a madman or something worse. You can shut him up for a fool, you can spit at him and kill him as a demon or you can fall at his feet and call him Lord and God, but let us not come with any patronizing nonsense about his being a great human teacher. He has not left that open to us. He did not intend to.[82]

One of the most wonderful, and hilarious testimonies of coming to faith in Christ is by the founder of the worldwide Vineyard Churches movement, the now deceased John Wimber. He was a late-night show musician in Las Vegas in the 1960s and 70s, drinking heavily and doing drugs. His marriage was falling apart, his life was in a mess. Someone advised him that he could get in touch with God if he watched the sunrise, so he drove out into the desert as the sun rose and prayed his first ever prayer: 'God help'. As soon as he got back to the hotel his phone rang and it was his wife Carol, from whom he was separated and facing divorce, saying they should give their marriage another go. John says he prayed his second ever prayer, 'At-a-boy God', who either smiled or rolled his eyes. The Wimber family began to attend church and a homegroup. But Wimber says he was getting increasingly frustrated and finally told the Bible study leader he wanted to stop. Why? Wimber remembers saying: 'All you guys talk about is Jesus, and I don't wanna talk about Jesus, I wanna talk about God.' The leader replied 'that's because you don't understand that Jesus is God'. Wimber replied, 'Where does it say that?'[83]

It took a while for the penny to drop, that Jesus is God with us. And at that final fateful supper, Jesus revealed it fully.

## SEE WHAT JESUS PREPARES

*'My Father's house has many rooms; if that were not so, would I have told you that I am going there to prepare a place for you? And if I go and prepare a place for you, I will come back and take you to be with me that you also may be where I am.'*

JOHN 14:2–3

Here is the basis and balm for the disciples' anxious hearts. Whatever troubles they will face, such are fleeting, transient, temporary. The valley of the shadow before them is not where the story ends, where the journey ceases. The best is yet to come. Eternity sets everything in perspective. They must trust in Jesus who is God, who is making room in his home for them to live with him.

It has often intrigued me why the Bible is almost silent in descriptions of heaven. This has led to all sorts of conjecture, flights of artistic imagination or worse, fabrications of visitations with numerous books claiming to be testimonies of people who went to heaven and came back – and who have little more to say than they sat on Pappa's lap and saw their old deceased relatives who were happy and the grass is very green.

What the Bible is discreet about, we should not presume upon. Whenever we read of people seeing visions of God in heaven – Isaiah, Ezekiel, Daniel, John – they collapse overwhelmed. Paul went to heaven and yet said: 'what no eye has seen, what no ear has heard, and what no mind has conceived – the things that God has prepared for those who love him.'* The Spirit reveals something of this to our spirit, but let us not diminish its glory by speculation.

I believe we simply do not have words or concepts to bear the weight of the reality of heaven. We simply do not have the experience on which to build an adequate analogy or correspondence.

We have some dear friends who paid for us to stay for dinner, bed & breakfast at the famed two Michelin star restaurant and hotel, *Le Manoir aux Quat'Saisons*. We had known of its reputation as one of the best Michelin restaurants in the world, led by the great chef Raymond Blanc. But to stay there and to eat there is an experience ordinary folk like us just don't have – it's something we watch others enjoying, on our TV. It is so far removed from anything Tiffany and I have been used to. We could never afford it, nor justify it if we could. But a gift given must be received, and it was an unforgettable, once-in-a-lifetime experience.

Everything was exquisite in every detail. The welcoming staff were attentive, kind, putting the uneasy at ease. They made us feel special. The stunning grounds with walled gardens, immaculate lawns, beautiful flower beds, vegetable gardens, ponds, sculptures, bronzes, vegetable and herb beds. Our room with the most sumptuous bed I've ever slept in, Italian marble bathroom with gold taps, champagne on ice, huge shower that worked at the right temperature immediately. Not a hint of dust or a tear in the wallpaper or a scuffed carpet. Then the meals – seriously, I wiped away a tear more than once – utterly exquisite, culinary perfection. I mean, what can be said of an intense red pepper and crab sorbet starter?

---

* 1 Corinthians 2:9.

Or the clearest consommé with truffle and wild mushroom and poached quail's egg. Or of a pistachio soufflé which, when explored, had frozen chocolate ice-cream in it. The intensity of flavour, the perfection of presentation, all served with grace by staff who are enjoying your joy, all in a sublime setting. And the wines – every one hand chosen to bring the best from the food; Château d'Yquem – crème de la crème. Unforgettable. Wonderful.

Yet, everything at *Le Manoir* I could find words to describe – indeed comparisons could be drawn with the best *humus* and pitta for a fiver, that I had eaten in the Old City of Jerusalem three days earlier. But of heaven, we are left virtually speechless. We have neither language nor experience to conceive and compare with the Father's House – *Le Manoir de Dieu*.

After 48 hours we left *Le Manoir* to return to our vicarage and it seemed a little more shabby, a little more scruffy than it had before, and the stains and scuffs and dust and tiredness were a little more obvious. King David said, 'I will dwell in the house of the LORD forever'.* And so will we who trust in God and trust also in Jesus.

## SEE HE GETS US THERE

*'I am the Way, the Truth and the Life. No one comes to Father except through me.'*

JOHN 14:6

Few of us will ever gain access to the Queen, or the President of the USA. People of power and importance protect and preserve themselves from ordinary folk, understandably. But the extraordinary reality of the Christian faith is that we have access to God Almighty, he wills it and has made it possible. There is a way to the Father, God is available, God is accessible, God has not cut himself off from us, or cut us off from him, forever. God who dwells in unapproachable light will make

---

* Psalm 23:6.

himself available through Jesus whose death will be the door. Whilst no limit or restriction is placed on who may come to God, the way is unique and exclusive. It is only through Christ – no one can come any other way – no other route or path or door is available. There is only one door into the throne room of God and only the Father's Son can open the door to the Father's Mansion.

## JESUS IS THE WAY

The Bible uses the concept of being lost to define the human condition when separated from God the Father. It is thus no surprise that many carry a deep and profound existential sense of lostness. And this theme echoes through culture – consider the long-running and eminently successful multi-series drama simply called *Lost*. Or think of the opening biographical line in Dante's 'Divine Comedy':

Midway upon the journey of our life
I found myself within a forest dark,
For the straightforward pathway had been lost.
Ah me! how hard a thing it is to say
What was this forest savage, rough, and stern,
Which in the very thought renews the fear.
So bitter is it, death is little more;[84]

Think about the Coldplay song *Lost*, or the tragic suicide of the rocker, Chris Cornell, whose album was called *Lost and Found* and who, in several songs, expressed being a lost cause. I once watched a programme in which the famous three Michelin star chef, Marco Pierre White, bought an old railway sign that said, 'Lost Property'. He commented, 'I think I'll put that over my study – I've been lost all my life'. How sad. We are made in the image of God, for God, to be with God in paradise. And we are not what we should be, where we should be, with whom we should be. JRR Tolkien powerfully expressed this in a letter to his son Christopher:

> Certainly there was an Eden on this very unhappy earth. We all long
> for it, and we are constantly glimpsing it; our whole nature at its best
> and least corrupted, its gentlest and most humane, is still soaked
> with a sense of exile.[85]

Everyone is lost until they are found and brought home. Jesus is the way.

## AND JESUS IS THE TRUTH

In the presidential debates in the USA for the Republican Primaries in 1999, a journalist asked the candidates who was the greatest philosopher who ever lived. Bush answered 'Christ'. Candidate, Alan Keynes, who earned a PhD in Philosophy from Harvard, countered, 'Philosophers search for truth … Jesus IS the Truth.' Our postmodern culture does not care much for objective truth (though the proponents still want their pay packet to mean what it says and not less than). But in our culture, everything is subjective, pragmatic, pluralistic, relativistic – as the infamous novel put it *Shades of Gray*. We don't even know black from white anymore. Problem is, who do we trust? How do we build a basis for law, justice, ethics – life together?

The band the Manic Street Preachers had a prophetic song for our times, *This is my truth tell me yours*. This loss of truth as a moral, spiritual foundation brings anxiety and chaos. Without truth the rule of the jungle takes over and the fiercest lion rules. The birth of sin was a lie against God. The demonic deceived Adam and Eve from the start twisting the truth of God – and having acquiesced with the serpent's commentary on God and stepped into chaos, deception has been a mark of mankind ever since. The extent of mankind's truthlessness will be seen shortly when on trumped up charges Jesus is tried and executed – Pilate will obfuscate '*quid est veritas* – what is truth?' – he would fit well in our world now. And finding no charge against Jesus, he still crucifies him. He could not handle the truth. Dogs don't lie. Humans do.

Jesus witnesses to the truth. Jesus embodies the truth. About God, about us, about life. And Jesus said, 'you will know the truth, and the truth will set you free'.*

## JESUS IS LIFE

Existence is never enough. We want to live before we die, but do we? We seek life here and there, in achievement, acquisitions, intimacies. Few find these substitutes to last. Most fail to live and live afraid to die. Shakespeare's Macbeth says melancholically,

> 'Life is but a walking shadow; a poor player that struts and frets his hours upon the stage and then is heard no more ... a tale, told by an idiot, full of sound ... and signifying nothing.' [86]

But Jesus offers us satisfied life:
'I am the bread of life. Whoever comes to me will never go hungry, and whoever believes in me will never be thirsty'.

Jesus offers us eternal life:
'I am the resurrection and the life. Whoever believes in me, though he die, yet shall he live'.**

So, how do we access this way to God, this truth, this life in Jesus. Take hold of Jesus. Believe in Jesus. Put your trust in Jesus.

My friend, the well-known and much-loved North of England evangelist, Robin Gamble, says he only has three sermons: 'Come to Jesus,' 'Come back to Jesus,' and 'Come closer to Jesus'.

Jesus bids us, 'come'.

---

* John 18:38; John 8:32.
** John 6:35; John 11:25 (ESV).

# CHAPTER 12

# HE KEEPS A PROMISE

*And he gave us bread and wine to join with
him and with one another*

*I will lift up the cup of salvation
and call on the name of the LORD.*
PSALM 116:13

Tiffany, my wife, collects small coffee cups. She has done for decades.
We have dozens of styles and colours displayed on our Welsh
dresser. Recently as we browsed an antique shop, Tiffany spotted
some art deco cups and saucers that she liked. I had no objection
but was surprised by her rationale, which was, that our others look
old fashioned. Most are actually less than twenty years old – so in an
ironic modernization of her collection she buys some seventy-year-
old Art Deco cups. But some cups never go out of fashion.

In this chapter I want us to think about the timeless cup of cups.
The cup of the Lord. The Lord Jesus, on the night he was betrayed,
he took the cup, gave thanks to God, and gave it to them, saying,[*]

> 'Drink this, all of you. This is my blood, God's new covenant poured
> out for many people for the forgiveness of sins.'

MATTHEW 26:27–28 (THE MESSAGE)

In the Old Testament, the cup is understood figuratively and
symbolically. It represents three things:

[*] 1 Corinthians 10:21.

- an individual's fate: 'my cup and my portion' (Psalm 11:6, ESV)
- divine wrath: 'from the hand of the LORD the cup of his wrath' (Isaiah 51:17); 'from my hand this cup filled with the wine of my wrath' (Jeremiah 25:15)
- divine blessing or salvation: 'my cup overflows' (Psalm 23:5); 'I will lift up the cup of salvation and call on the name of the LORD' (Psalm 116:13).

These three motifs of the cup as an individual's fate, the cup as God's wrath and the cup of God's blessing underlie the drama of the Last Supper. Jesus took the cup of *fate* – his fate which was to embrace our fate of judgment; he blessed it and blessed God and gave the cup to the disciples. Jesus took the cup of God's wrath and he gave the cup of God's blessing to his disciples. Jesus' blessing on the fruit of the vine reverses the age-old curse of Adam, of the fruit of the tree. Unless we drink in faith the blessed cup of salvation Jesus offers us, we will drink the cup of his wrath.

The Gospel is contained in this cup. This cup is foremost among the church's treasures, the most sacred of her rites, the centerpiece of her worship. The *sine-qua-non*, without which we are not the people of God. This cup is the mystery that makes sense of everything. A few moments in time that catch us to eternity.

Let us begin by considering our terms. The Last Supper, re-enacted and represented has been variously designated.

- Eucharist – Jesus took the cup and gave thanks. The Greek word is *eucharisteo*. This meal was first called eucharist in the *Didache*, a late first century handbook for Church life and worship. This name recalls Jesus giving thanks to the Father but also invites us to give thanks.

- The Lord's Supper – this is the title Paul gives, and it conveys something of the fact that the Lord is the host who lays the table and invites us to the feast of grace.

- Breaking Bread – this is the term given in the Acts of the Apostles. Breaking bread is also a generic term for having a meal and this sacred remembrance was often an integral part of general meals together, only later developing into a formal independent liturgical service.

- Mass – this Catholic title originates from the last words uttered by the priest in the Latin Eucharist *Ite Missa est* – 'Go, the dismissal is made'. It is sadly ironic that 'go away' has become the name for the meal in which Jesus says 'come, sit and dine with me'.

- Holy Communion – this is a term derived from Paul's letter to the Corinthians: 'the cup of blessing' is communion, *koinonia* with the blood of Christ, as the bread is with the body of Christ.[*] This term became popular after the Reformation. 'Holy' underlines its sacredness while 'communion' emphasizes the union with God and each other.

Most traditions, whatever they term this meal, agree it is a sacrament – a sacred moment – which imparts the grace of Christ. A sign that is both a sign of Jesus and grace that assigns us. God gives himself to us in the cup of wine and bread in more than words, propositions, and ideas. Some seem to reduce this to a mere memorial, a time to contemplate and think about his death – but I believe there is something powerful in and of itself, and far more than a proposition to consider. God gives himself in a form for our senses to perceive: sight, touch, smell, taste all are employed when we come to the cup – it is visceral, tangible, real, we ingest. We drink the cup, we taste the wine and eat the bread and in the physical we receive the blessing

---

[*] 1 Corinthians 10:16–17.

that is spiritual. Jesus said 'take and drink' – not 'take and think'.

I think in these days of postmodern suspicion of the authoritative word, signs and symbols are even more important, and the cup speaks a better word.

St Augustine described the sacrament as 'an outward and visible sign of an inward and invisible grace'.[87] In similar vein, Number 25 of the Church of England's doctrines in her 39 Articles, says by the sacrament God 'works invisibly in us and not only quickens us, but strengthens and confirms our faith in him.'[88] A few Protestant traditions would reject this understanding of the sacrament as a superstition and see the cup as only a visual aid, a memorial, helping us to remember the cross. But they sit at odds with most of the church for most of her history – and if only a sign to recall, why are we told to 'take and drink'? When Jesus said, 'this is my body' and 'this is my blood' he meant more than 'this is a picture, a symbol, a representation' – no, he identifies himself with it. This is the mystery of the sacrament, but just because we cannot grasp it, we must not allow our incredulity to define our theology.

In the Anglican service of the eucharist, after the prayer of consecration, the priest invites all who are thirsty and all who are hungry for God to come and feast, saying:

> Draw near with faith.
> Receive the body of our Lord Jesus Christ
> which he gave for you,
> and his blood which he shed for you.
> Eat and drink
> in remembrance that he died for you,
> and feed on him in your hearts
> by faith with thanksgiving.[89]

This holds together the four key features of the communion brilliantly:

- our faith in him
- his giving himself to us in bread and wine
- a memorial of his death
- a thanksgiving.

Incidentally, as with the term 'mass' so also the term 'hocus pocus' comes from the old Latin service when the priest declared the words of institution, '*Hoc est Corpus mea*' – 'This is my body', whereupon a server would ring a bell to signify the notion that the elements in the hands of the priest, now mystically changed from bread into the real corporeal body of Jesus. With respect, this is not a view I find consonant with Scripture.

The sacrament is mystical but it's not magical. The communion elements do not change physically and substantially into the very DNA of Christ, but we do believe they change spiritually, by the Spirit. Jesus is present in a particular way, and God's blessing is in the cup to those who drink in faith. The seventeenth century Anglican poet and priest, George Herbert wrote,

> Only thy grace, which with these elements comes,
> Knoweth the ready way,
> And hath the privy key,
> Opening the souls most subtle rooms;[90]

Through these elements, the grace of Christ leaps through our body to our souls – this heavenly food feeds us at the core of our being. The church has often become very philosophical and metaphysical – probing who can celebrate, how they do it, what words, what gestures, what type of bread, what exact moment is consecrated, what change occurs, what to do with the wine and bread after. The Bible addresses none of these questions and we should not be hung up over them, though we need to do everything decently and in order. The church believes these natural emblems, become supernatural, by faith – they strengthen our union with Christ, they bless us on the journey.

Richard Wurmbrand was the Romanian pastor imprisoned by the communists for a total of fourteen years, in which he suffered greatly and was tortured repeatedly. He stayed faithful through it. He recalled that the one thing he missed the most was communion. Wurmbrand said that there was no bread or wine for communion – the only food available was filthy rotten cabbage. But the Lord said 'Nothing, is what I used to create the heavens and the earth and everything in them.'[91] So he and his prisoners with only their imaginations celebrated communion. No fine liturgies, no silver gilt chalice, no paten, no priestly robes, no choir anthems – no bread, no wine. Just memory, faith, imagination and desire – and the grace of God descending to feed them and bless them.

## WHY DO WE DO THIS? BECAUSE JESUS SAID '*THIS DO ... DO THIS*'

What an extraordinary thing – Judas has left the meal and gone into the shadows of the night to work his worst. Within hours Jesus will have been betrayed, seized, abused, mocked and tried. Before the sun sets a second time he will have been scourged and cruelly slain – and taken on his shoulders the sins of the world. And yet, his thoughts are not for himself but for his disciples and he offers them comfort and commentary on the unfolding events. Oscar Wilde wrote 'love is a sacrament'[92] – I prefer to say 'sacrament is love'.

*Jesus instituted this for us* – Jesus ordained it. He took, he blessed, he gave it to them, saying 'take, eat, do'. The church didn't invent this. Twice Paul emphasized, 'I received from the Lord what I also passed on to you.'*

*And Jesus Interprets this* sacrament as a Gospel event, and offers us four keys to understand it:

---

* Luke 22:8; 1 Corinthians 11:23; 1 Corinthians 15:3.

## PASSOVER

*'I have eagerly desired to eat this Passover with you before I suffer.'*
LUKE 22:15

This occurred at Passover, the feast when the Jewish people gathered to remember their deliverance from slavery in Egypt. The lamb slain, the meal eaten, the blood painting the door frames, the angel of death passing over. The Passover meal symbolized God's wrath on the Egyptians and God's salvation for the Israelites. In just the same way, this Last Supper would signify the cup of God's wrath drunk by Jesus and the cup of salvation drunk by the disciples.

## COVENANT

*'This is My blood of the new covenant.'*
MATTHEW 26:28 (NKJV)

In the Old Testament, a covenant, or binding agreement, made between God and humans, would be sealed or ratified with blood. God made a covenant with Abraham to make him a people, a father of a whole nation, and to give this people a place. The covenant was ratified by shed blood, God walking between the halves of the sacrifice.

The Old Testament prophesied a new covenant, a new Spirit, a new law written on their hearts, a new knowing of God. And Jesus is instituting this new covenant, and ratifying it, sealing it in his blood.

## SACRIFICE

*'poured out for many for the forgiveness of sins.'*
MATTHEW 26:28

Jesus is the Lamb of God whose blood takes away the sin of the world. Jesus is the substitute for sinful humankind whose death will satisfy the justice of God. So this cup speaks of forgiveness. Communion is designed for sinners in need of forgiveness.

It is a strange irony that many times people exclude themselves from communion because they feel 'sinful' or 'not worthy'. The devil wants to keep us from this grace. Indeed, even the church made up rules and placed obstacles to keep people at a distance from the cup. Like the need to fast for hours beforehand, or to go to the priest for confession, or to not sleep with your spouse. All religious nonsense. This is a cup for sinners to come and imbibe grace.

I made a new friend. He is a professional bodyguard and bouncer. He spoke colourfully, not realising I was a vicar. Then he asked my job, and I said 'I'm a priest'. He spoke colourfully again, then apologised again. I shared a little of my story. And he interjected, 'Can a person really be forgiven? I haven't murdered anyone, but I've done things. Can you be forgiven?' I put my hands on his shoulders, 'Yes, you can, you really can, anyone, of anything, even murderers. Jesus forgives us, it's what he does.'

Jesus took the cup of wrath so we could drink the cup of salvation.

The fourteenth century mystic, Julian of Norwich, had a series of divine visions: the fourth, she titles 'Dear worthy blood of Jesus', writing,

> this precious and plenteous worthy and dear blood descended down into hell, burst forth her bonds and delivered all there who belonged to the court of heaven. The precious plenty of his dear and worthy blood overflows the whole earth and is ready to wash from sin all creatures …[93]

## A FORETASTE OF HEAVEN

> *'I tell you, I will not drink from this fruit of the vine from now on until that day when I drink it new with you in my Father's kingdom.'*

MATTHEW 26:29

In the SAS camp at Hereford, on Training Wing, the wall is covered with old photos of SAS troopers – on mountains, in jungles and in war zones – all there to inspire the new recruits. On the wall is a quote: 'When living in the present, and planning for the future, remember that which connects you to the past.'

Communion is a present grace, that connects us to a past event and causes us to anticipate a wonderful future hope when we feast with Jesus in heaven.

## HOW DO WE RESPOND?

### JESUS INVITES US TO COME

In Rublev's famous and beautiful Icon, three figures sit at a table. They probably represent the Lord and two angels who met Abraham (Genesis 18) but many have taken the three to symbolize the Holy Trinity. The three persons sit at the table, but there is a space at the table in front of the viewer – and there on the table a cup. The hands and posture of all three focus the eye on the cup, and inside an image of a Lamb. And space at the table, for the observer to draw near and sit and sup.

### COME CONSCIOUSLY – JESUS SAID 'DO THIS IN REMEMBRANCE OF ME'.*

As we come we 'remember him', we fix our thoughts on his eternal glory, creator of the universe, who sustains all things by his powerful word. We consider his miraculous incarnation, humility, humanity, ministry, his free offering of himself, hours of agony, plundering hell, glorious resurrection, ascension, his return and reign. This is about our Saviour who took the cup of wrath so we could drink the cup of blessing – let our thoughts linger on him. Though serious, it

---

* 1 Corinthians 11:25.

is also joyous. As the cup of blood and bread of life touch your lips, kiss the Son.

## COME BOLDLY – THIS IS NOT A MEAL WE COME TO WHEN WE FEEL HOLY AND SPIRITUAL

Jesus gave it to his disciples knowing that, within a few hours, they would all betray him. As we said above, this is a sinners' cup. Love bids us welcome – there are no hurdles but faith and need. There is a beautiful welcome prayer originally by John Hunter in a book of liturgy from 1880. It has been adapted many times, but its heart remains the same: come.

> Come to this sacred table,
> not because you must but because you may,
> Come, not because you are strong,
> but because you are weak.
> Come, not because any goodness of your own gives you a right to come, but because you need mercy and help.
> Come, because you love the Lord a little and would like to love him more.
> Come, because he loved you and gave himself for you.
> Come and meet the risen Christ, for we are his Body.

## COME REGULARLY

*'do this whenever you drink it in remembrance of me'*

1 CORINTHIANS 11:25

*'On the first day of the week we came together to break bread.'*

ACTS 20:7

In the medieval church, this meal became more magic than sacrament and priests celebrated it several times a day and laity never. Some Protestant traditions restrict it to only once a year. John Calvin encouraged it weekly. John Wesley when chaplain in Oxford, wrote an article called 'The duty of constant communion' and encouraged us to partake as often as we can and recommended four times a week and on saints days. It was Charles Spurgeon's custom, whether at work or on holiday, to partake of the Lord's Supper each Sunday. He often testified that the more frequently he obeyed his Lord's command, 'This do in remembrance of Me', the more precious did his Saviour become to him.[94]

## COME REVERENTLY – JOYFULLY BUT NOT LIGHTLY

Just think of a wedding, of the bride and groom, they draw near in joy and reverent awe. Paul warns that some have become sick and even died because they did not recognize the Body – these are sacred things, this is Holy Ground. It is not, as I once heard a church worker say, an occasion to 'eye up talent in the queue' – nor, having received communion, a time to read emails on our phones or catch up with the person next to us. Let us prepare ourselves to receive, to reflect afterwards, and come with all the dignity this affords and honour the sacred.

## COME BELIEVINGLY

Feed on him in your hearts by faith[95]

It is not the hands of the priest that make the sacrament a grace – it is not your good deeds and religious devotions, its merit is in itself, that Jesus drank the cup of God's wrath to bless the cup of our salvation. In faith alone, O lamb of God I come.

## CONCLUSION

One day a parcel arrived for me at the Parish Centre. It was from a new friend I had met by chance in a coffee shop. He was a remarkable man, a hero, a true servant of society and church. His name was John Allport MBE, QGM, BEM. He had been honoured with medals for bravery and national service. Opening the bubble wrap I found a dented, grey, base-metal communion chalice. Attached was a note from John saying that he had been given this by the colonel of the regiment and felt I, as a priest should own it. A covering note explained it had been used by Royal Artillery Regimental Forces Chaplain Reverend GT Briggs at Dunkirk, on D-Day and every day after as the Allies pushed through Europe until victory in Germany. Amidst the hell of war, Jesus was present ... the covering note said this: 'many thousands, of all nations, who across Europe during WWII received comfort in its priestly administration and sacred ministry.' Every day this cup brought grace and mercy and Jesus joining them through the miles of trauma and tragedy to ultimate victory.

This cup is my most prized personal possession – this cup of our Lord is the world's most prized possession.

# CHAPTER 13

# HE TAKES THE BLAME

*And scheming men sat in judgment on him*
*And they condemned him and handed him over*

*The Apostles' Creed, an ancient ecumenical summary of Church*
*foundational doctrine, states succinctly that Jesus:*
*suffered under Pontius Pilate,*
*was crucified, died and was buried;*
*he descended to the dead.*[96]

These fifteen words, imprinted on memory by constant repetition, by generation after generation of Christians across the nations, roll too easily off our tongues. Just as Atlas strained to hold up the heavens, we strain to comprehend and convey the immensity of the reality behind these propositions. Here is the unfathomable and inexpressible love of God, whose breadth and length and height and depth are beyond knowing.

## JESUS' DEATH IS FOUNDATIONAL

Jesus' death is foundational to our faith and our revelation of God. The cross is creedal. The cross is the *sine-qua-non* of our faith. It is the primal verity, the first of our truths. Neither incidental nor accidental, the cross is the crux of the matter. St Paul wrote from his chains that he 'resolved to know nothing while I was with you except Jesus Christ and him crucified.'[*]

[*] 1 Corinthians 2:2.

The Christian faith is cross-shaped. All religions have their divinities and their sacred places, inspired texts and holy prophets, spiritual devotions, and righteous actions, but only Christianity has a cross as a gate to life. Only Christianity has a God who becomes flesh to suffer at the hands of wicked men in order to save those wicked men from their sins.

Yet strangely many who would call themselves Christian have become numb to God's passion – church has become little more than a community, or their choir, or their custom, and they have lost its core. One Sunday, my father was preaching at a local Open Brethren church that my sister attends. Dad was preaching on the cross of Christ. One chap sat next to my sister, not knowing she was the preacher's daughter, and at the end of his sermon said dismissively, 'Oh that's all old ground'. It is old ground – but it is the only ground we have to stand on. The only solid ground that can take the weight of our sin; the holy ground where heaven touches earth, the battle ground where the devil is undone, the healing ground where sin is covered and heaven offered. To borrow Paul Tillich's term, the cross is the 'ground of all being', of all that constitutes us.[97]

To declare that we believe Jesus was crucified is not just an assent to an event – it is to summon that event into your present and to have it frame your life. The late second century theologian Tertullian wrote, 'At every forward step and movement, at every going in and out, when we put on our clothes and shoes, when we bathe, when we sit at table, when we light the lamps, on couch, on seat, in all the ordinary actions of daily life, we trace upon the forehead the sign [of the cross].'[98]

# JESUS' DEATH WAS HISTORICAL

*Suffered under Pontius Pilate*

Jesus' death was not abstract, metaphysical, ahistorical, philosophical. It is not a Greek Tragedy, a poignant play, a meaningful myth, a universal symbol, a metaphor in which we search for a correspondence of meaning. The cross was a real event, in real time, in a real place where a real person really endured hell. For us. That suffering was 'under Pontius Pilate' – the Roman Prefect of the province of Judea, serving under Roman Emperor Tiberius, AD26–AD36. All four Gospels attest to Pilate's central role in the crucifixion, as do the greatest historians of the first century: Israel's Josephus, Philo of Alexandria and the Roman Tacitus all mention Pilate as Judea's Prefect. There is also archaeological evidence from the first century of standing stones set up in his honour.

We know Jesus was crucified. We know who crucified Jesus, giving the order, to bow to the Jewish authorities, to keep the peace, despite finding no charge against him. We know where he was crucified, his cross hoisted on the rocky knoll outside the city gate. We know when Jesus was crucified, at the feast of Passover, early on that Friday, after a mockery of a trial at Herod's palace at 7am. We know that he was tried by Pilate at 8am, crucified at nine in the morning (the third hour according to the Gospel of Mark), and that he breathed his last at three in the afternoon.[*]

In the late second century, the Roman historian Celsus made an attack on Christianity. In one of his arguments, he claimed that had Pilate really killed God's Son and not just an insurrectionist, surely the gods would curse him with a terrible fate – but they didn't, so Jesus obviously wasn't God's Son. But Celsus understood nothing of the God of Jesus Christ nor of the power in forgiveness that Jesus

---

[*] Mark 15:25 (ESV); Matthew 27:45.

prayed in the throes of death, as the prophet Isaiah saw, 'he bore the sin of many, and made intercession for the transgressors.' From the cross he prayed, 'Father forgive them, for they know not what they do.'* Could it be that even Pilate, the one who ordered this suffering, or who sealed the suffering, might himself also be forgiven? Of course. One church tradition, presented by Tertullian, tells us Pilate 'himself also in his own conscience was now a Christian'.[99] The Ethiopian church claim Pilate became a Christian and a martyr and declared him a saint! It wouldn't surprise me – it would be just like God to save Pilate, rather than condemn him.

## JESUS' DEATH WAS BRUTAL

*he suffered ... was crucified, died*

Jesus suffered. We will never be able to plumb the agonies of his betrayal, beatings, mockings, injustice, ignominy and agony – and all at the hands of those he came to love and save. Mark writes, 'Again and again they struck him on the head with a staff and spat on him. Falling on their knees, they paid homage to him.'** They humiliated him, with their mock homage, a reed as a staff, and the cruel crown of thorns pressed through his flesh. CS Lewis captured something of this in Aslan's scourging,

> They surged round Aslan, jeering ... 'Puss, Puss! Poor Pussy' ... and 'would you like a saucer of milk?' ... The shorn face of Aslan looked to her braver, and more beautiful, and more patient than ever ... 'Muzzle him' said the witch. And even now, as they worked about his face putting on the muzzle, one bite from his jaws would have cost two or three of them their hands. But he never moved.[100]

---

* Isaiah 53:12; Luke 23:34 (ESV).
** Mark 15:19.

Then they led him out to be crucified. Today people wear crosses, two thousand years ago crosses wore people. No one recovers from the cross. The cross was designed for slow, public, torture. The Romans didn't invent crucifixion, but they perfected it as a form of torture and capital punishment and used it as a thing of terror, a threat to quell any notion of rising up to challenge Rome's control. The Roman historian Cicero said it was the cruelest and most disgusting penalty: 'the very word "cross" should be far removed not only from the person of a Roman citizen, but from his thoughts, his ears, and his eyes.'[101]

In 1986, *The Journal of the American Medical Association* published a series of articles on torture. The first article, by a theologian and a medic, was called 'On the Physical Death of Jesus Christ' by Dr William Edwards and Wesley Gabel. Below is a summary:[102]

## THE SCOURGING

This was no clinical execution – Jesus' death was drawn out by vicious torture. The scourging 'was intended to weaken the victim to a state just short of collapse' and it satisfied the blood lust of sadists who pleasured themselves with the sight of blood and screams of pain. The condemned man 'was stripped of his clothing, and his hands were tied to an upright post. The back, buttocks, and legs were flogged by two soldiers ...' with short whips made up of 'several single or braided leather thongs of variable lengths, in which small iron balls or sharp pieces of sheep bones were tied' which 'would cause deep contusions ... and cut into the skin and subcutaneous tissue. Then, as the flogging continued, the lacerations would tear into the underlying skeletal muscles and produce quivering ribbons of bleeding flesh.'

## THE ROUGH IRON NAIL

Driven or hammered by one hand into another man's hands would 'crush or sever the rather large sensorimotor median nerve. The stimulated nerve would produce excruciating bolts of fiery pain in both arms ... Adequate exhalation required lifting the body by pushing up on the feet and by flexing the elbows and adducting the shoulders. However, this manoeuvre would place the entire weight of the body on the tarsals and would produce searing pain. Furthermore, flexion of the elbows would cause rotation of the wrists about the iron nails and cause fiery pain along the damaged median nerves ...' Finally, after enduring hours of unrelenting agony, what would finally kill the crucified would be cumulative trauma, shock and suffocation, or acute heart failure. Our term 'excruciating' is taken from the Latin word *excruciatus*, or 'out of the cross'.

The cross is the criteria against which pain is measured.

However, the physical sufferings of our Lord were not the worst of it – the loveliest life the world has ever known smashed against a tree, marred and disfigured, a face from which men hide their faces – that is not the worst of it. Others regularly endured the same physicality of brutality at the hands of the Romans – five thousand slaves who rebelled with Spartacus were crucified in 71BC. The greater suffering, and utterly unique suffering, was that 'God made him who had no sin to be sin for us'; God 'laid on him the iniquity of us all'; he became accursed for us hanging on a tree; he bore our sins in his body on the tree. And Jesus endured estrangement from his Father – a greater tearing than that of his flesh, 'My God, my God, why have you forsaken me?' So great the horror as the light of the world is murdered, that the sun itself bows to the darkness that covered the earth at the beginning, the chaos is come again.[*]

[*] 2 Corinthians 5:21; Isaiah 53:6; Galatians 3:13 (NLT); 1 Peter 2:24 (ESV); Matthew 27:46; Luke 23:44.

God did not design the cross of Christ – that was the despicable handiwork of the demonic – but God consigned Jesus to the cross. Jesus himself, as the cross rushed to meet him, as he is arrested, says 'this is your hour – when darkness reigns.'* But, as CS Lewis said, there was a deeper magic at work – and God in his sovereignty, chooses to use this evil suffering, of the willing sacrifice of his Son, as a satisfaction for his justice against sin, and as an atonement to cover the sins of the world. It is a mystery and a marvel that cannot be fathomed, only received.

## JESUS' DEATH WAS A SCANDAL

The Apostle Paul called the message of Christ crucified a 'stumbling block [Greek: *scandalon*] to the Jews; and foolishness [Greek: *moron*] to the Gentiles.'** The cross is *scandalous* and *moronic* – how could anyone affirm belief and hope in this obscene vile act as the means of their personal salvation?

It is an offence, in so many ways.

- There is a *moral offence*: how can God's wrath be such as to require satisfaction in blood?
- There is an *ethical offence*: how can it be just for an innocent to pay for the sins of the guilty?
- There is a *philosophical offence*: how can the particularity of one man in one place at one time be said to have universal and eternal ontological effect?
- There is *theological offence*: how can God's Son assume sin and die?
- There is an *existential offence* – how dare you say I am personally so guilty that only God's son dying for me will suffice to cover my guilt?

* Luke 22:53.
** 1 Corinthians 1:23.

- There is a *religious offence* – how dare you say my religious acts and devotions are insufficient to atone for my sin, that they are as filthy rags, even?

It is little wonder then that this most sacred event is confusing to many, despised and rejected by others.

The philosopher Nietzsche protested, indeed he railed his whole life against Christianity and especially the cross. In his book *The Antichrist*, which he wrote in 1888, he ranted:

> I call Christianity the one great curse, the one great intrinsic depravity, the one great instinct of revenge for which no means is venomous enough, or secret, subterranean, and *small* enough – I call it the one immortal blemish upon the human race.[103]

Nietzsche defined himself as Dionysus against the crucified, he mocked Jesus on the cross saying God was a spider on the wall, and yet strangely he signed his last letters as simply 'the crucified'.

The pop star Madonna was probably responsible for making the cross a fashion accessory in the 1980s, just as institutional religion went out of fashion. This crafted and clever provocateur mocked the symbol of the cross and took the definitive symbol of the sacred, clashing it with the symbol of the seductive. When asked why she wore a cross, she replied, 'crucifixes are sexy because there's a naked man on them.'[104] Later on in her career, decades later, she staged a mock crucifixion of herself in a show, singing from a cross, wearing a crown of thorns. Provocative, offensive, subversive. Of course, many will say it's just art, theatre, play, and there are no 'no-go areas' – even the most sacred. Zealous atheist Richard Dawkins tweeted his scorn and derision, following the appeal of a British Airways stewardess to be allowed to wear her cross at work: 'Such fun being a victim. Waaaaah. I'm allowed to wear my crossy-woss only INSIDE my BA uniform. Where only God can see it.'[105]

Paul writes, 'many live as enemies of the cross of Christ.'* Knowing that the cross is the death knell to the demonic and the gateway to eternal life – spiritual antichrist forces seek to debase it, to dismiss it. Nevertheless, this scandal, this moronic demonic event – is God's power of salvation for all who believe.

## JESUS' DEATH WAS MYSTICAL

The Apostles' Creed is carefully circumspect. It presents no commentary, no soteriology, no theory of atonement. The creed states the facts of the event – you will not find in her a transactional analysis of substitution or an algebraic equation for salvation. There is silence over exactly what occurred in those three hours of Jesus on the cross and afterwards, up until the third day of resurrection. The writers were content to live with not a little mystery in the economy of God. The creed states: 'he descended to the dead' but what does this mean? Some see in this 'descent' a nod to the sole New Testament reference touching on those intervening hours between cross and resurrection:

> For Christ also suffered once for sins, the righteous for the unrighteous, that he might bring us to God, being put to death in the flesh but made alive in the spirit, in which he went and proclaimed to the spirits in prison.**

How are we to understand this 'descent to dead' and proclamation to the spirits in prison? There are several views: some regard this as referring not to Jesus' mission in the grave, but as a reference to the Spirit of Jesus in the Old Testament, who preached to and through the prophets who are now awaiting his glorious revealing and their liberation. Others understand the descent to the dead as an idiom conveying the very real and full entering of Jesus into the

---

* Philippians 3:18b.
** 1 Peter 3:18–19 (ESV).

reality of death – drinking the earthly cup to its deadly lees. Some regard this as speaking of the liberating of those who were deemed righteous under the old covenants – like Noah and Abraham who were waiting for Jesus to come to paradise and take them to heaven. It has been suggested that Jesus here is giving the unrighteous dead a second chance, an opportunity to hear the Gospel and be saved. Lastly some see this as Jesus addressing the demonic spirits, chained in hell, a rubbing their nose in the glory of his death. Any, all, or none of these may be right. But the lack of confirming Scripture means here we must hold those hours in the grave a mystery, and not be too dogmatic about our interpretation.

Notwithstanding cross references and apostolic commentary, this verse from 1 Peter 3, and the notion of the descent of Jesus into Hades, became hugely popular in antiquity and in the medieval era, although the preoccupation with it and their conclusions were largely rejected by later Protestants. It's fair to say there are more artists' paintings made of it than there are apostolic Scriptures written about it. The idea, widely called the 'harrowing of hell', is drawn from the reference to Jesus' descent to the dead and is powerfully stated in the fifth century Gospel of Nicodemus: Christ breaks down the doors of hell, binds and tramples upon the foul spirits, and, taking Adam by the hand, conducts the saints to paradise.[106]

What occurred when Jesus lay in shrouds in a tomb is shrouded from us and we must be careful not to speculate – in the New Testament the Apostles emphasized Jesus' death and his resurrection. Notwithstanding all this, the very real truth conveyed in the 'harrowing of hell' paintings, and the associated literary depictions, is of the very decisive victory of Jesus – his triumph over death and his deliverance of those captive to sin, death and hell.

## JESUS' DEATH WAS, FOR US, PERSONAL

We say, 'I believe', and in doing so, we are not merely giving assent to a past event, we are embracing and owning it for ourselves. He died for me. The famous Swiss theologian Karl Barth called us to,

> Look once again to Jesus Christ in his death on the cross. Look again and try to understand that what he did and suffered, he did and suffered for you, for me, for all of us. He carried away our sin, our captivity, our suffering, and did not carry it in vain …[107]

When you next say the Creed, don't rush over these words – subconsciously after each phrase insert 'for me': He suffered under Pontius Pilate (for me) was crucified (for me) died (for me) was buried (for me) and, hallelujah, he rose again for me. There are over forty verses in the New Testament, which specifically emphasize Jesus' death 'for us', in the place of us, as a substitute for us. Consider just these few:

- He gave his body and his blood, *for us* (Luke 22:19–20)
- He died *for us*, whilst we were still sinners (Romans 5:8)
- He became sin *for us* (2 Corinthians 5:21)
- He became a curse *for us* (Galatians 3:13)
- He loved us and gave himself up *for us* (Ephesians 5:2)
- He tasted death *for us* (Hebrews 2:9)
- He was a ransom *for us* (1 Timothy 2:6)
- He suffered *for us* (1 Peter 3:18)
- He is the atoning sacrifice *for our* sins[*] (1 John 2:2).

What a great cost for our forgiveness and reconciliation with God. How utterly extraordinary – God thinks you are 'to die for'. My friend Mark, who served for seventeen years with the SAS, tells the story of how his former troop were involved in the liberation of the British

---

[*] Emphasis on 'for us' and 'for our' mine throughout.

military peacekeepers who were taken hostage in the terrorist camp in Sierra Leone. Having entered the hostile camp and while securing it, the SAS located the hostages and released them from their locked cell. As they made their way to the Chinook helicopter, one of the liberating troops was shot in the back. He was lifted onto the helicopter with the freed hostages – but died immediately. As the Chinook took off, the rotor blades caused the rear of the helicopter to lift up first and tilt the helicopter forward. The dead trooper's lifeblood ran down the helicopter onto the hostages feet, who were sat at the front. Mark commented to me: 'the freed prisoners knew then the cost of their freedom.' That noble SAS warrior gave his life to give the hostages life. The cross was the cost of our forgiveness. Jesus' death the price of our life.

God's love is cruciform – it is cross shaped. In love God chooses the injustice of Jesus' death to satisfy his own justice, and to win us for himself. You are desired by God, loved by God, and he went to hell and back for you. Eugene Peterson, whose life and writings have inspired the worldwide church, went to be with the Lord in 2019. At his funeral his son Leif said his dad Eugene only had one sermon. Words that stuck in his own heart when his dad snuck into his bedroom at night to whisper over him as he snuggled down to sleep:

*God loves you*
*God is on your side*
*He is coming after you*
*He is relentless.*

Yes, and we know that, because Jesus suffered under Pontius Pilate, was crucified, died and was buried – for you.

# CHAPTER 14

# HE LOOKS AND HE SEES

*And his executors said 'Truly, this man was the son of God'*

*Ecce Homo*
JOHN 19:5

Look, see, behold, observe the man. The infamous words, translated from the New Testament's Greek to Latin, of Pilate, as he displays the flayed Jesus to the crowds who had bayed for blood. Jesus now stands naked, wearing only his own blood and Herod's robe as a covering. But although they tried their very best, the Roman soldiers could not beat the dignity or glory from this beautiful man. In moments Jesus will carry the cruel cross that will be the throne of his death. And yet, *Ecce Homo* invites Pilate: look, see, behold, observe the man, the Son of Man, the man for others. There are many artists who have dared to attempt to portray the sufferings of Jesus in these moments and behold the man, behold, *Ecce Homo*. But as I behold the wounded one, I have mused what he himself beheld, what of *Ecce Homo*. What if Pilate had said this in the vocative,[108] addressing Jesus, 'Man, look'. What would Jesus see?

A few artists portray a Jesus with open eyes, wistfully looking up to heaven, or pained, staring down at the ground, his thoughts elsewhere beyond the present torment. Most artists portray Jesus with eyes closed,[109] Jesus searching in his mind through the searing pain for his Father, hiding from the derision and scorn of his mockers and murderers, those who schemed his death, and even those who, days before, welcomed him, arms open and palms waving and shouting 'Hosanna!', now shouting 'Crucify him!'

## SEEING JESUS WHO SEES US

In 1930, the Spanish painter Elias Martinez went on holiday to Borja Spain, and while he was there, he painted a portrait of Jesus, 'Ecce Homo', on the local church wall. His Jesus, wearing a crown of thorns, stared heavenward. Over the years the damp took its toll and the plaster on the wall began to flake and the portrait to disfigure. In 2012 a local resident and amateur artist, 80-year-old Cecilia Giménez, took it on herself to restore the fresco. She did her best, and then went on holiday herself. A visitor saw it and uploaded it on to social media, where it went viral. When Cecilia got home, she found the small town full of tourists and reporters, all interested in her and her restored painting. Most mocked the image as bizarre, even sacrilegious. One BBC correspondent described it as a 'crayon sketch of a very hairy monkey in an ill-fitting tunic'.[110]

Yes, Gimenez's restoration significantly changed the original. Yes, she was not a gifted artist and her Jesus was ugly. Yes, her image brought worldwide ridicule and mockery in a thousand memes, and a comic opera was even made of the story. But previously, no one visited the town to see the stylised Victorian chocolate box image. But since the portrait was restored, 200,000 pilgrims have come to see it. The town's economy, which had been suffering, with 300 recent job losses, was turned around, and, as one commentator put it, 'the town, if not the painting, was restored'[111] by those who had come to see Jesus.

But for me, Gimenez's naïve image improves in one respect over the original, whose Jesus gazes into thin air. Gimenez's portrait of Jesus stares straight at us – he sees us as we see him. He does not turn away, turn inside, turn wistfully upward. He sees us. And his gaze holds ours. We behold the man, and the man beholds us. We see his agony and he sees those for whom he willingly endures it. His gaze holds ours. We want to look away but we cannot. We are seen by the one who sees us.

In Genesis 16 we meet Hagar running away from her mistress Sarai because of ill treatment. Hagar is met by the angel of the Lord who informs her she is pregnant with Ishmael and must return home. But there is a promise of blessing: thereafter, Hagar gave another name to the Lord who had spoken to her, *El Roi*,

> *'You are the God who sees me,' for she said, 'I have now seen the One who sees me.'*

GENESIS 16:13

In a beautiful Gospel cameo early in Jesus' ministry, Philip goes to his friend Nathanael and says:

> *'We have found the one Moses wrote about in the Law, and about whom the prophets also wrote – Jesus of Nazareth, the son of Joseph.'*
> *'Nazareth! Can anything good come from there?' Nathanael asked.*
> *'Come and see,' said Philip.*
> *When Jesus saw Nathanael approaching, he said of him, 'Here truly is an Israelite in whom there is no deceit.'*
> *'How do you know me?' Nathanael asked.*
> *Jesus answered, 'I saw you while you were still under the fig-tree before Philip called you.'*

JOHN 1:45–48

## WHAT DID JESUS SEE FROM THE CROSS?

Normally our focus is on Jesus *on* the cross, but what was Jesus' focus *from* the cross?[112] Hoisted aloft, his head perhaps at a height of ten feet, through his blood-bleary eyes, Jesus saw.

- Jesus saw the *centurion* and the *Roman death squad* who, moments before, with clinical, efficient brutality, had, almost nonchalantly, killed him. He was no one to them, just another criminal, they were under orders, doing their job, another day at the office, and they sat down and cast lots for his clothes (Matthew 27:36, 54).

- Jesus saw the *two thieves* on either side, one mocking and spitting out scorn, the other bowing his head, and asking to be remembered in heaven (Luke 23:39–42).
- Jesus saw his *mother and John the beloved* and in his own agony, was still taking care of things, telling them, 'this is your son' and 'this is your mother'. Even as he's dying, he's caring for them (John 19:26).
- Jesus saw *the women* who had followed him – they didn't deny him, they followed him faithful to the end – weeping. Their bitter tears would turn sweet (Luke 23:27; Matthew 27:55).
- Jesus saw the *disciples* who had denied him, who stood at a distance ashamed, and he loved them. They thought it was all over. Little did they know (Luke 23:49).
- Jesus saw the *chief priests and pharisees and scribes* jeering, and leading the crowds in mocking him: 'He is the King of Israel; let him come down now from the cross and we will believe in him' (Matthew 27:41; Mark 15:30–32).
- Jesus saw the *crowds*, who had welcomed him just days earlier, waving palms and shouting 'Hosannah!', now wagging their heads, deriding him, but some mourning (Matthew 27:39–40; Luke 23:27; Luke 23:48).

Then there are others that Jesus saw – who would that be?

- Jesus saw the *walls of Jerusalem and the city gate* – probably the gate of Ephraim, that he had come out of, and people were coming and going, some stopping to stare, reading the sign above his head, others, dropping their heads and scurrying away, some oblivious (John 19:20).

- Jesus saw the *Temple* and the priests slaughtering the daily sacrificial lamb, the *Tamid*. This lamb was offered twice a day, at 9am and 3pm, the hour at which Jesus was crucified and the hour Jesus died.* During these two hours of sacrifice, Jewish tradition states that special prayers, the 'Eighteen Benedictions' were offered – including prayers for redemption, forgiveness of sins, the coming Messiah, the resurrection of the dead. As they prayed, as the two lambs were offered, Jesus saw and understood.[113]

- Jesus saw the *Tower of Antonia* where the Romans were garrisoned and possibly where Pilate had interrogated him, mercilessly scourged him and sealed his fate.

- Jesus saw the *Old City of David* where his kingly ancestor ruled Israel's kingdom, where so much blood would be shed, including his own, and to where Jesus will return to rule on David's throne.

- Jesus saw the *Mount of Olives* where, just the night before, that seemed a lifetime ago, Jesus was crushed in grief, betrayed with a kiss, arrested and seized. Where he chose not to summon a legion of angels to his rescue, but to where he will return with myriad on myriad of angels.

'... and Thou look'st towards me, O Saviour, as Thou hang'st upon the tree.'[114]

JOHN DONNE

Jesus' gaze was not held only by this natural vista. Jesus from the cross saw around the world and through time; and he saw everyone for whom he was there. The prophet Isaiah saw Jesus six centuries before and prophesied: 'When he sees all that is accomplished by his anguish, he will be satisfied.' The writer of the letter to the Hebrews

---

* Numbers 28:1–8; Exodus 29:38–42; Mark 15:25; Mark 15:33–37.

says of Jesus 'for the joy set before him endured the cross' – but what was the joy set before him? Surely it was the goal of Golgotha, the redemption of the world from sin, death and hell, the reconciliation of all humankind to the Father, the restoration of all things under his lordship.*

Yes, even in the trauma and the throes of death there was the joy of what he had won. The joy of seeing his Apostles take the Gospel of his death and resurrection from Jerusalem, to Judea, to Samaria and to the uttermost ends of the earth. The joy of seeing his Bride, the church of Christ, grow from a handful of frightened followers to a mighty army waving banners – glorious through time, prepared for eternity. The joy of seeing his kingdom come on earth as in heaven and the hostages of evil set free and the damage of evil renewed. The joy of seeing the multitudes on multitudes of every language, tribe and tongue worshipping the triune God. The joy of seeing you, dear Reader, come to know him and revel in his love. Yes, he saw you from afar and he loved you.

## WE NEED TO FOLLOW THE GAZE OF GOD FROM THE CROSS

The early Apostles followed the gaze of God, then followed through and went to those who the Lord saw from Calvary. An early and rather unlikely legend says the twelve Apostles cast lots and divided up the world to determine who would go where. According to tradition:

- *Andrew* saw as far as Russia, Turkey and Greece where he was crucified.
- *Thomas* saw as far as Syria and eventually India and Madras, where he was speared to death.
- *Philip* saw as far as Carthage in North Africa where he was stabbed to death by the Roman proconsul for converting his wife.

* Isaiah 53:11 (NLT); Hebrews 12:2.

- *Matthew* saw as far as Persia and Ethiopia where he was martyred.
- *Bartholomew* saw as far as India and Armenia and Southern Arabia where he was skinned alive.
- *James* saw as far as Syria and was clubbed to death in Israel.
- *Simon* the Zealot saw as far as Persia where he was sawn in two.
- *Matthias* who replaced Judas saw as far as Syria where he went with Andrew and was martyred by fire.
- *John* saw as far as Ephesus – and was imprisoned on Patmos.

There are many and contradictory traditions surrounding the Apostles and their destinations and eventual deaths. Ancient churches in ancient countries claim various ones as the bringer of the Gospel. Reliability and verifiability are shrouded in time and hagiography. But go they did, and far and wide, telling of the height and depth and length and breadth of the Gospel. Those who saw Christ followed his gaze to the nations with the Gospel and through that the church of Christ was founded.

And for two millennia, people have gazed at God's Son on the cross, and followed his gaze to the world, and taken the Gospel there. There are more Christians in the world in 2018 than there were total inhabitants in the world in 1948 – his offspring possessing the nations. When I was training for the ministry at theological college in the early 1990s, I made friends with a Korean mission leader, Dr Stephen Hah. He founded and oversaw a huge ministry for renewal and missionary expansion, and sent several thousand missionaries into the East. One day at college, I went to his rooms in college and, after knocking on his door, walked in, without waiting to be invited. I will never forget what I saw – Stephen Hah was on his knees, holding a blow-up globe, eyes full of tears, having been praying for the nations. Is it any wonder that God has used him so?

But many who Jesus saw remain unseen and unreached. To borrow Mary Poppins' phrase, we often 'can't see past the end of our nose'.[115] Often, we are preoccupied with ourselves, we are myopic, short sighted, focused on ourselves, our family, our next holiday, our work, or our pension. The one thing Jesus couldn't see on the cross was himself. A consumerist spirit has turned the church in on itself. Many will happily fly to California for a renewal conference to obtain a blessing – but how many will fly somewhere on mission to be a blessing? Nowhere does the New Testament say 'go on pilgrimage' – its presupposition is that we will go on mission. Pilgrimage is personal, now there's a place for that. Jesus' counsel to the church in Laodicea is one we could well heed, get 'salve to put on your eyes, so that you can see.'* The saintly Edinburgh professor, James Stuart Stewart, challenges me:

> Shall I, as a Christian, be content to pursue the religious quest as a private hobby and to develop my own spiritual life; or shall I concern myself personally for those outside and take upon my heart deliberately the whole world's need for Christ. No man with the New Testament in his hand, can have a moment's hesitation about the answer. 'What I live by' declared St Augustine, 'I impart'.[116]

Count Zinzendorf, a wealthy young German aristocrat, visited a gallery in Düsseldorf in the early eighteenth century, where he saw the painting *Ecce Homo* by Domenico Feti. In Latin script at the bottom are painted the words: *This have I done for you; now what will you do for me?* Zinzendorf was struck, as it were, by lightning, and gripped to the quick. Foregoing the flamboyant indulgent lifestyle usual for young men of his station, he chose a simple and humble way of life. He founded the Herrnhut community, built homes for

---

* Revelation 3:18.

persecuted Bohemian Protestants who led prayer meetings 24-7 for a hundred years, who formed hundreds of renewal groups over Europe, sent numerous missionaries to follow the gaze of God and take the Gospel of Jesus to the nations – establishing works in Germany, Denmark, Russia, Latvia, England, the West Indies; to the Inuit in Greenland, amongst the native Americans, the Copts in Egypt, and, with a special heart for the negro slaves in bondage in South America, to Nicobar, South Carolina and East India.[117]

This man saw Jesus, and saw what Jesus saw, and went. Behold.

# CHAPTER 15

# HE WINS

*And he had the last word as he pushed the stone away*

*But Christ has indeed been raised from the dead, the firstfruits of those who have fallen asleep. For since death came through a man, the resurrection of the dead comes also through a man. For as in Adam all die, so in Christ all will be made alive.*
I CORINTHIANS 15:20–22

In this book I have sought to present the expansive person and work of Jesus. It began with a working document of over seventy sermons as the basis for chapters, which would have been a very fat book indeed. I have whittled the seventy down to a modest twenty. But if I were forced to choose just one, I think it would be this chapter. This is the 'irreducible minimum' of the faith, what the Apostle Paul called 'of first importance'.* The Christian faith is not predicated on the perfect life of Jesus, nor the profound teaching of Jesus, nor the signs and wonders of Jesus, nor even the divinity of Jesus and his incomprehensible incarnation. The thirty years he lived in Galilee before beginning his public ministry are shrouded in mystery. Neither Jesus nor the Apostles invite us to probe them. His three years of public ministry are glorious and foundational for our living as disciples of Jesus and understanding the king and his kingdom, but they are not the goal, not the climax. The trajectory of all these is the cross and resurrection. The Gospels themselves focus their

---

* 1 Corinthians 15:3.

attention on the last few fateful days of Jesus in Jerusalem, and this is clear from their allocation of commentary: a third of the Gospel of Matthew, from chapter 21 to chapter 28; a third of Mark's Gospel, chapters 11 to 16; a quarter of the book of Luke, chapters 19 to 24; almost half of the Gospel of John, chapters 12 to 20. The Passion narratives make up over a third of the Gospels.

This is Jesus' destiny. This is the denouement of the Gospel. Christianity is a religion predicated on the death and resurrection of Jesus. His dying and rising were the purpose in his first coming. Jesus' coming, living, teaching and ministering were all utterly breathtaking, but they were not what saves us – if Jesus had ascended before the fateful events of the cursed tree and the empty tomb, then we would probably still have a Jesus movement, a new religion, for sure, but there would be no forgiveness, no salvation, no redemption, no reconciliation to God.

## THE DAY OF DAYS

After years of frustrating searching, on 4 November 1922, the famous Egyptologist Howard Carter discovered the entrance to the tomb of King Tutankhamun. Carter later described it as: 'The day of days, the most wonderful that I have ever lived through and … one whose like I can never hope to see again.' As Carter entered the tomb with his torch, the sponsor, Lord Carmarthen was standing above ground, and shouted down, 'Can you see anything?' Carter replied, 'Yes – wonderful things.' His light revealed the shining gold statues and fabulous jewels; and going further in, there was the now world-famed treasure, the golden enameled sarcophagus of King Tutankhamun.[118]

Two millennia ago, the disciples of Jesus went into the tomb where Jesus had been laid, and what did they see? Wonderful things. Things they did not expect and would never forget. But not golden statues, and not a bejeweled royal sarcophagus with a mummified king within. They saw nothing but an empty tomb and discarded grave clothes. They saw nothing. That nothing was the greatest thing. The King is risen. Treasure beyond comparison.

## THE EMPTY TOMB MEANS JESUS IS LORD

The devil wanted Jesus dead. Darkness hates the light and so did its best to snuff it out. The Romans wanted Jesus dead, a troublemaker who stirred up the people and could incite a riot. The Jewish rulers wanted Jesus dead, a king they did not recognize, who undermined their authority and shook the balance of power. Betrayed with a kiss, tried in a makeshift court on trumped up charges, stripped and humiliated, flogged and flayed half to death, marched out amidst the cries of the mockers, outside the city wall, despised and rejected, there they crucified him. There was only one way out of this drawn-out torture: death. And death would come, but it would take its agonizing time. From the abattoir of Golgotha, Jesus' carcass is tenderly taken to Joseph of Arimathea's newly hewn Garden Tomb. A giant stone is rolled across, sealed on Pilate's orders, with Roman troops to stand guard.

And that was that, the end of it, or was meant to be. And would have been, but God had other things in mind, as public theologian Tony Campolo heralded, 'But that was only Friday – Sunday's coming'.[119]

The Apostle Paul wrote that if Jesus is not raised, we would be without hope, dead in our sins, not saved and to be pitied above all others. But Christ has indeed been raised and the one who was raised is now reigning, 'he must reign until he has put all enemies under his feet ... for he has put everything under his feet.[*]

Feet function as a metaphor for authority. The ancients depicted their gods with their feet on the kings, and then the kings with their feet on the governing ministers, and their feet on the subjects. Feet

---

[*] 1 Corinthians 15:14–20, 25–27.

---

were a symbol of rule, power, and that which was beneath the feet was subject to that power.

Everything is placed under the feet of him who took a towel and washed the feet of his disciples. Can you imagine it? Consider Jesus' feet. The wise men from the east had knelt at them in wonder. They had nestled in the palm of Mary's hands and been kissed with tender love. Those feet that kicked the wood shavings in his father's carpentry room. Those feet that paddled in the shallows of Galilee. Those feet that strode upon the raging seas and calmed the waves. Those feet that walked the dusty road up to Jerusalem; that paced through the filthy cobbles of Jerusalem's bustling streets. Those feet that were kissed with tears and dried with hair, feet that were loved and anointed with precious nard. Those feet that felt the roots of the olive tree as he knelt and prayed in Gethsemane. Those feet that were pierced and pained and stained with his own blood. Those feet that trampled the winepress on the third day, the blood began to flow, those toes to tingle, and they wiggle and they swing over the chiselled stone bed, and they stand firm and strong on the stone floor – planted and supplanting the power of death and sin and the demonic.

## ONE CLEAR WINNER

In *Troy*, the movie adaptation of Homer's *Illiad*, two armies gather in battle. The Greek King Agamemnon suggests a single combat between their respective armies' greatest warriors to prevent a needless massacre. The winner will decide the fate of the war. If the Thessaly champion wins, the Greeks will go home – if the Greek champion wins, Thessaly will come under Greek rule. The Thessalian champion Boagrius steps forward and Achilles is summoned to fight for the Greeks. Before the gathered armies, the two champions meet each other in mortal combat. Achilles runs to meet the Thessaly giant, who quickly responds by hurling his spear. It misses and he swipes with his sword. Too late. In one quick strike Achilles slays the enemy champion. Achilles then walks up to the rest of the shocked Thessalian army and asks: 'Is there no one else? Is there no one else?' No one moves. None comes forward. No other adversary, no other champion, no one else brave enough or fool enough to face this invincible foe. Achilles is the victor, to the Greeks goes the day.

Christ at the cross faces the devil and wins. At dawn on Easter morning Jesus cries: 'Is there no one else? No other adversary? No other debt, no other charge? And none came forward. The demons retreat to the shadows. The devil's worst was spent. The day is Christ's, to the victor goes the spoils! The stone is rolled away and up he arose, victorious and glorious, with an angelic shout that thundered through heaven. On Easter Sunday there was one clear winner – Jesus – and one clear loser – the devil.

The devil miscalculated. In that most famous boxing match in Zaire in 1974, between Mohammed Ali and George Foreman, 'the Rumble in the Jungle', the heavier and more powerful Foreman took the fight to Ali, pounding him for seven rounds. People watched in agony and awe as punch after punch, blow after blow landed on Ali's body. His corner and the crowd were shouting to Ali to move off the ropes, to avoid the relentless thunder from Foreman. But Ali had his own game plan. For seven rounds Ali faced his foe, toe to toe, and soaked up every punch Foreman threw. By the seventh round Foreman had given all he had: his strength was spent, his lungs gulping for air, his muscles stiff with lactic acid. But Ali, although battered and bruised, was not beaten. It was only Friday. Sunday was coming. In the eighth round, Ali came off the ropes, and dancing like a butterfly and stinging like a bee, with a few well-timed blows, knocked Foreman down and out.

On Good Friday the devil had Jesus on the ropes, and threw at him everything he had, seeking to sniff out the light of the world. By three in the afternoon, the Son of Man lay dead on a gibbet. The demonic thought the day was his. But that was only Friday – Sunday was coming. Jesus soaked up all the spite-filled evil the demonic had, he also satisfied all the demands of divine justice – it was finished, *tetelestai*, it was full and sufficient. And on Easter Sunday morning, with a violent earthquake that shakes heaven and earth as the stone is rolled away, Jesus rises again, and the demonic is given a knock-out blow. His body, 'sown in dishonour, it is raised in glory; it is sown in weakness, it is raised in power.'*

In *Lord of the Rings*, Gandalf, who has returned victorious after descending to the depths joined in deadly battle with the Balrog. But he triumphs and returns transformed and Aragorn says to him:

> you are our captain and our banner. The dark lord has Nine. But we have One, mightier than they: the White Rider. He has passed through the fire and the abyss, and they shall fear him. We will go where he leads.[120]

What a glorious image of Jesus who compels our allegiance – he is the white rider who has descended into the depths and fought and defeated the great demon king, he has overcome death and risen and is robed glorious – he is our king and we will follow him.**

## THE EMPTY TOMB MEANS SINS ARE FORGIVEN

*And if Christ has not been raised, your faith is futile; you are still in your sins.*

1 CORINTHIANS 15:17

But he has, and he is!

Beneath the satanic schematic of death, a deeper magic was at work. The dark materials of betrayal and brutality and murder become the substance God reworks to recreate humankind's destiny. This is the great marvel, a great mystery of our faith. The beautiful innocent lamb freely took the punishment for our sin, the

---

* 1 Corinthians 15:43.
** Revelation 19:11–13.

estrangement from God. God turned away from his Son, to turn aside his wrath from us, to turn his face toward us. God as holy and righteous judge must punish human sin. If he doesn't, he is not holy, good, righteous and just. But he is all this, and so he does satisfy justice, and in the free volitional sacrifice of the Son of God who assumes the representative Son of Man, Jesus becomes the sacrifice for sin, the substitute in our stead, and the satisfaction of divine justice. This side of eternity we will never understand – some even protest – but for those who believe, this is life.

But how can we know if our sins are forgiven, whether Jesus' death in our stead was sufficient and an acceptable offering pleasing to God? Well, because he is God, and he knows what is required. Yes, but how can we know? By Jesus rising from dead. This was God's declaration and demonstration that his death was sufficient and that we are forgiven.

On Good Friday we stood, guilty as charged. On Easter Sunday we are acquitted, of all charges.

There is an ancient Jewish myth set in the time when Israel was wandering in the desert – worshipping at the travelling tabernacle, where God's glory dwelt in the ark of the covenant. Around God's tent was a fence of posts and skins. Each year the High Priest would offer a sacrifice for the sins of all the people on the Day of Atonement. But how would people know if the sacrifice was acceptable, whether their sins were actually forgiven? The Jewish myth says that the people hung scarlet rags on the posts that demarcated the sacred tabernacle area. And when the priest emerged from the holy of holies in the tent, if God accepted the sacrifice for the sins of the nation and forgave their sins, it was said that the red cloths turned white. Though their sins had been red as scarlet, they were turned white as snow. On Good Friday we must imagine that all our scarlet sins have been hung on Jesus. But on Easter Day, as Jesus shatters death and rises again, our sins red as scarlet, are turned white – forgiven, forgotten, forever.

I love the ancient words of Archbishop Cranmer, later martyred for his Gospel faith, found in the 1662 service of Holy Communion. Carefully and precisely they attest to the effect of the cross of Jesus, proven by the resurrection:

> All glory be to thee, Almighty God, our heavenly Father, for that thou, of thy tender mercy, didst give thine only Son Jesus Christ to suffer death upon the Cross for our redemption; who made there (by his one oblation of himself once offered) a full, perfect, and sufficient sacrifice, oblation, and satisfaction, for the sins of the whole world ...[121]

When God broke the seal on the tomb and rolled the stone away, it was God's seal that the death of Jesus was efficacious for us. And that he has rolled our sin away.

I mentioned before that I had the privilege at Easter of preaching to the pilgrims at the Garden Tomb in Jerusalem. The nations gathered from Scandinavia, America, France, India, Nigeria, Mongolia, Korea, Indonesia. It was extraordinary – many dressed in their tribal or national costumes, they spoke different languages, they worshipped in their own cultural styles – shared one faith. And at the heart of that faith is the shared experience of Jesus as Lord and sins forgiven.

Among the varying glorious groups of pilgrims, the Indonesians stood out to me, and I went and sat next to them for half an hour. They worshipped most beautifully, and prayed aloud passionately with many tears of personal gratitude and also tears of pain as they interceded for their own nations' salvation. But they also carried visual aids, prophetic symbols to focus their devotion and speak of their faith. One lady held a silver silk-covered cushion and on it was a golden globe of the earth and the words 'Jesus King of kings'. A young man held a beautiful white lambskin pelt with the words 'Behold, Jesus the Lamb of God who takes away the sin of the world'.

# FINALLY, THE EMPTY TOMB MEANS DEATH IS DEFEATED

*Christ has indeed been raised from the dead, the firstfruits of those who have fallen asleep. For since death came through a man, the resurrection of the dead has also come through a man. For as in Adam, all die, so in Christ all will be made alive.*

1 CORINTHIANS 15:20–22

Death came through sin. Before Adam's sin there was no death. We inherit our life from Adam and we also inherit our death. Death is the consequence of sin.* Sin separates us from God who is life. And so, sin is our undoing, our un-living, our death. But Jesus died and took the penalty for our sin, he faced our judgment, he died our death, he took our penalty, our punishment, and in so doing put death to death.

Philip Larkin was haunted by the fear of death all his life. He has been called 'the Graveyard Poet' as so many of his poems are drawn to the shadows. His father had died relatively young of cancer aged sixty-three, and Larkin was tormented that he too would die young of cancer. Solomon said 'that which a man fears shall come on him',** and it was true for Larkin, who also died at sixty-three, also of cancer! His death phobia haunted him, formatted his personality, making him a bitter old man from a young age. He was self-centered, sexist, anti-Semitic and unable to commit to marriage. The fear of death sucked all the joy of life out of him. Look at these lines of poetry that he wrote:

Death is unpreventable, all streets in time are visited …
Death. So permanent and blank and true.
That lies just under all we do.   (Ambulances)

* Romans 6:23.
** Proverbs 10:24, my paraphrase.

153

At death you break up; the bits that were you

Start speeding away from each other for ever
With no one to see; its only oblivion, true   (The Old Fools)

Till then I see what's really always there:
Unresting death, a whole day nearer now,
Making all thought impossible but how
And where and when I shall myself die.
Arid interrogation: yet the dread
Of dying, and being dead,
Flashes afresh to hold and horrify. (Aubade)[122]

Eric was a well-known local character, an Oxford rogue. He had
lost most of his friends because of stealing from them. He couldn't
help himself. I liked him a lot and we often had a cuppa and chat.
He was not religious, but always respectful and always engaged me
in a religious discussion that would often seem to come around to
the subject of death. Eric would invariably initiate it, then become
uncomfortable and end it. One day when I went to his stall, he
handed me a Salvation Army songbook dated 1906 that he had
saved for me. He read out the strapline on the cover: 'Are you ready
to die?' I told him I was and asked if he was. He made a joke. Few
people are ready to die. Last year, he died. Of cancer. He only went to
hospital when he was already terminally ill, and some kind friends
insisted and took him there. The hospital sent him home and he
died not long after. He had told folk they were not to tell me he was
ill. Maybe as a priest I represented and confronted him with death.
But they told me anyway. And then he asked to see me. It was a
privilege, I was able to share a little and he let me pray for him. I
should have said more and done more. I don't know if he was ready
to die and meet God.

Death is the universal human experience; every community has
its cemetery. Death casts a long shadow over our lives – people want
to live, not die. Anthropologist Ernest Becker wrote, 'the idea of

death, the fear of it, haunts the human animal like nothing else – it is the mainspring of human activity'.[123] But it need not be now. For Jesus is risen, death is defeated, life is offered to all who hold onto Jesus. Adam brought death to the world by eating of the fruit of the tree; Jesus brought life to the world, by dying for our sins, on a tree.

CS Lewis wrote,

> Jesus has forced open a door that had been locked since the death of the first man. He has met, fought and beaten the King of Death. Everything is different because he has done so.[124]

Exactly. And Everything is different.

Where Oh death is thy sting! Spent. Death died the day Jesus rose. If we look to Jesus in his death for our sin, and trust in Jesus in his resurrection to life, we are united with Jesus, and the merits and benefits of his death for us, pass to us. Forgiveness and life evermore.

## THE RESURRECTION MEANS:

- The resurrection means that God is at the helm of history.
- The resurrection means Jesus can be taken at his word.
- The resurrection means that Jesus is Lord over death, Lord of Life.
- The resurrection means that sins were fully atoned for at the cross.
- The resurrection means Jesus' substitution was sufficient sacrifice for all.
- The resurrection means that eternity has been ushered in, begun.
- The resurrection means the days of the demonic are numbered.
- The resurrection means those who hope in Jesus will rise with him.

David Watson, the great evangelist of the 1970s and 80s, was diagnosed with terminal cancer. As he was dying, he wrote a book called *Fear no Evil*. He wrote, 'The Christian doesn't prepare for death, but for life'.[125] One of the outstanding spiritual guides and greatest Christian leaders of the past century was Eugene Peterson. He wrote many books and *The Message* translation of the Bible. At the heart of his lived faith was the Easter story. Eugene had a cross in every room of his house. In his book *Living the Resurrection* he wrote 'what I want to do is rediscover our resurrection centre'[126] – a life lived with the reality and power of Jesus' resurrection at the centre. He would have agreed with CS Lewis, 'death and resurrection are what the story is about'.[127] Eugene lived – and died – well. His son said that as he hung in the thin place between life and eternal life, between earth and heaven, he was talking to people not in the room but present to him (saints in heaven?) and he prayed in tongues, the language of heaven, and among his final words were, 'Let's Go'.

I picture Jesus coming, the King of life and Conqueror of death, walking to meet his beloved faithful Eugene, and taking him by the hand to walk him through the valley of the shadow into unquenchable light and life.

# CHAPTER 16

# HE GIVES SECOND CHANCES

*He did not turn away when we turned away but kept advancing toward us, open armed*

*When they had finished eating, Jesus said to Simon Peter,*
*'Simon son of John, do you love me more than these?'*
*'Yes, Lord,' he said, 'you know that I love you.'*
*Jesus said, 'Feed my lambs.'*
JOHN 21:15

Almost three decades ago I went to theological college to train for the Anglican ministry. My very first assignment was to write a detailed study of the Greek text of John 21:15–19, paying particular attention to the subtle differentiations between John's use of paired words: sheep and lambs (*arnia* and *probaton*), feeding and tending (*boskein* and *poimainein*), love and love (*agape* and *phileo*). I got so bogged down in the subtleties in the text, that I missed the point. I failed to see the wood for the trees – so intrigued was I by the subtle nuances of the Greek language that I missed the message. Sadly, rather a lot of theological study can be a bit like this. I am a keen amateur photographer, but some photographic commentators spend all their time counting pixels, studying photos to see how much chromatic aberration or edge blurring or noise there is, and failing completely to stand back and see the image and composition!

I have often wondered subsequently, whether my wise old Greek tutor – Margaret Embury, Biblical scholar and four-foot female

Yoda – was trying to teach us more than our first lesson in Greek hermeneutics. Was she perhaps seeking, right at the start of our preparation for ordained ministry, to get us to understand the very essence of Christian leadership, indeed, of Christian discipleship, that is contained in this passage? Now, this discourse between Peter and Jesus was not held in Greek, the language it is recorded in in Scripture. It would almost certainly have been in Aramaic. But the inspired writer, presumably retelling what he heard, or perhaps what Peter told him subsequently, records this in Greek, and we must assume what he has recorded conveys the weight and sense of the original discussion.

## FLUSH OR WASH?

This is the first proper conversation between Peter and Jesus since the night Jesus was betrayed by Judas, arrested by the religious authorities and abandoned by his disciples. That dark night Peter denied Jesus, just as Jesus said he would; he denied knowing and having anything to do with Jesus, and he did it three times.[*] In Hebrew idiom, the number three represents perfection, totality and completeness, so Peter doesn't merely obfuscate, he completely denies Jesus. In this passage,[**] the resurrected Jesus meets the disciples back at Galilee. He has sent them there to lie down in green pastures and restore their souls after the trauma of Jerusalem. One dawn, after an unsuccessful night fishing – Peter is a rubbish fisherman by the way: we only meet him fishing twice and both times he catches nothing – Jesus comes to them. And instructs them to cast their nets on the other side. And, as had happened once before, as at the beginning, they haul in a huge catch. Peter wraps his clothes around himself and jumps into the sea. Most people take their clothes off to get wet, they don't put

[*] Luke 22:54–62.
[**] John 21.

them on – most fisherman catch fish too. Peter is a funny one.

After giving them a hearty breakfast, perhaps with the smell of the 'charcoal fire'* reminding Peter of that fateful night when he betrayed Jesus, while stood warming himself at another charcoal fire, Jesus takes Peter for a walk along the shore. And here, in the very place where Peter first encountered Jesus, forsaking all to follow him, Jesus pointedly addresses Peter's threefold denial. Not with the intention of rebuking him but seeking to restore him. Peter denied Jesus three times – here Jesus asks Peter three times to affirm his love. Each affirmation of love receives a re-commissioning of Peter to Apostolic service. Jesus aids Peter to undo, erase, recant, repent, and be restored. Jesus wants forgiveness, not failure, to mark Peter's life from now on. Sure, Jesus could have started again, found a replacement for Peter – I would have – but Jesus is much more gracious, forgiving, hope-full and he would rather restore than replace.

I was teaching at a church leaders' conference and in part addressing the themes of grace. One evening, while paying a visit to the loo, my signet ring slipped off my finger and fell in the toilet. Unfortunately, I had just done the business (number two) and my ring was buried in the day's detritus. I instantly knew my options: either to flush my ring away and claim insurance and buy another one, or to reach into the mess and rescue my ring. This ring had too much personal and sentimental value to flush it away! And it was also a seal engraved with the Lamb of God symbol – how could I flush such away? And so, I reached in, and unable to see it, rummaged around in the mess until my fingers felt something hard and cool amidst the soft and warm. I must have looked a strange sight to the many pastors in the large hotel toilets, as I exited the cubicle, filthy hand, ring held triumphantly, arm filthy, and proceeding to scrub myself neurotically for half an hour. Christ had the choice, to

* John 21:9 (ESV).

flush Peter away in his sin, or to reach in, and rescue, and clean and reappoint.

## DO YOU LOVE ME?

Three times Peter denied Jesus, three times Jesus elicits a profession of devotion. Before Peter can face the future, Jesus needs to deal with and heal the past. Each time Peter responds 'Yes, Lord ... you know that I love you', it's as if the stake in his soul placed by his denial is surgically removed. Peter's threefold denial is not the last word. God's grace makes space for new words, new affirmations of faith and not denial from Peter – and God speaks gracious words, tender words, restoring words, loving words. Jesus asks '*agapas me*' – of course, the evidence is that he doesn't, this superlative of loves, this agape love, is the love Jesus shows at Calvary, the love which Jesus said was greater than none – of laying down your life for your friends.* Peter denied Jesus – good friends don't do that, let alone those who love deeply. It is patently evident he didn't love Jesus with this love. Peter can only reply offering a lesser, lighter weight love (*phileo*) – a brotherly, family love. He can't measure up to the self-sacrificing *agape* love which Jesus showed and is owed – who ever can? But remarkably, it is enough. Jesus doesn't expect from us what he gives to us. He knows of what we are made. And each time Peter replies in the affirmative, albeit with diminutive love, Jesus kisses him with a commission: 'Simon son of John, do you love me?' ... is followed by 'Feed my lambs.' And 'Take care of my sheep.'**

Maybe some reading this can identify with Peter. You have really messed up. You have known the Lord's presence, intimacy, call, and yet under the pressure of temptation or trial have denied him, failed him. Maybe even 'three times', seriously, irrevocably, completely. Grace trumps sin. Grace triumphs over our failure if given to Jesus.

* John 15:13.
** John 21:15–17 (ESV).

The evil one wants accusation and condemnation to be the final word spoken over our lives – but grace makes way for restoration and for re-commissioning.

One of the world's great modern gurus of church growth has offered as a key axiom for leadership the notion of rewarding high-performers and removing underperformers. In many ways this makes perfect sense – invest in who and what is working, not who and what is not. Don't waste time on wasters. And one might even find certain Biblical texts to support such a view, perhaps the parable of the talents. But here in this narrative of Peter's restoration and re-commissioning, Jesus employs the opposite axiom. Grace for those who hit rock bottom. Jesus rewards this underperformer. The leader who has proved unfaithful, unreliable, who denies Jesus not once, not twice, but three times in as many hours – this fickle faithless follower is made lead Apostle.

Peter later went on to write, 'love covers a multitude of sins'* – God's love for us and our love for God. Sin and failure he can deal with – it's only the absence of any turning to God in love which brings exclusion and ultimate rejection, leaving us to ourselves and our sin. What stands out starkly here is that love is the all-determining criteria for leadership, for Apostleship, for discipleship. Jesus didn't go to hell and back to make us his slaves – Love redeemed us to be lovers. The distinguished Biblical professor, Leon Morris, once wrote that loving Jesus is the basic qualification for Christian service. Other qualities may be desirable, this love is completely indispensable.[128]

Sadly, church is full of people who want to feed sheep, but who don't love the Shepherd. Countless clergy who can barely mutter the creed for perjury, and who know nothing of Calvary love and love for Calvary. I have met them – ministers who love the ministry, but don't know the Master. Theologians who love theology but don't love

---

* 1 Peter 4:8.

Theos. In the process for becoming ordained, I was sent for numerous interviews, assessing my suitability for the ministry because, frankly, it wasn't immediately evident. Intelligence, vocation, psychological profile, emotional stability, marriage, gifting, personal story – all these were put under the scrutiny of examining chaplains. But not once was I ever asked 'Do you love Jesus?' The sublime Anglican Ordination service with its brilliant questions and responses asked publicly of those being ordained, that proffer themes that frame ministry, never ask whether the ordinands love Jesus. But Jesus didn't ask Peter anything about his gifts, abilities, talents, experience for the role, whether he earned a good degree, held a good pedigree, looked good in a cassock, had the right Myers Briggs psychological profile and was the right sort, had done his Belbin analysis on team functions to see how well he got on with others. No, just one question, put three times, 'Do you love me?'

The most effective disciple is not the most educated, most gifted, best connected, but the most passionate about Jesus – the one who glows and overflows with love for Jesus. There is nothing more attractive nor effective than a saint in love with their Saviour. Passion breeds passion, indifference breeds indifference.

It is well known that the Welsh Revival began in early 1904 in West Wales and was indebted to the preparatory prayers and ministry of Evan Roberts. What is less well known is that the revival broke following an incident with a teenage girl called Florrie Evans. One Sunday she went to the Pastor of New Quay, Cardiganshire, Rev Jenkins, for spiritual counsel saying she longed for spiritual joy and peace. He encouraged her to surrender to the lordship of Christ and submit to the leading of the Holy Spirit. She went away and did just that, handing over her life to the Lord. And God visited her. The following week she attended chapel and asked to give testimony in church. As she stood up, she simply said, 'I love Jesus with all my heart.' The Spirit came, wooed by this platform of public devotion. One by one those present surrendered to the Lord.[129]

Many wept, convicted of sin and their cold hearts. God came upon that congregation and God's Spirit swept through that country. Young Florrie Evans travelled widely with Evan Roberts, fanning the flames. The church was renewed, the community transformed, and an estimated 100,000 new members, converts, were added to the church in just six months.

It's strange but true, the one thing Jesus asks for, the one thing Jesus is looking for, is Peter's love. The Dutch Theologian, Abraham Kuyper once wrote, 'Even the heart of God thirsts after love.'[130] The first and greatest commandment, on which all the others hang, indeed, on which all the others are mere commentary, is not a prohibition, it's not a 'Thou shalt not'. It's an expression of affection, invitation, embrace, welcome, of longing for intimacy:

> Love the LORD your God with all your heart and with all your soul and with all your strength.
>
> DEUTERONOMY 6:5

If the greatest commandment is to love God, then it follows the greatest sin is to *not* love God. The greatest transgression is to withhold our affection from Jesus. Love fulfills the law. This is what Jesus wants of us, he wants us. He wants us to *love* him. 'Simon, do you love me?' is the question that confronts us all, and true worship is loving Christ, in word and deed and a life poured out and obedience.

Father Paneloux, in Albert Camus' *The Plague*, states, 'the love of God is a hard love, it demands total self-surrender,'[131] and total surrender is what Peter would, after this, give. When he repeated his third affirmation, *'you know that I love you'* Jesus proceeded to tell him that just as he was dressed and led by others as a child, so he would be tied and led by others where he did not want to go as an old man.* This was a prophecy that indicated Peter's eventual

---

* John 21:18–19.

arrest and death as a martyr: refusing to deny Christ he would be crucified upside down, during the reign of Emperor Nero. Peter had denied Christ, but he would eventually die for Christ. And it was his love for Christ that would be both the cause of his death and his willingness to endure it. No doubt the breathtaking love of God for him, experienced in part by Jesus' forgiveness and restoration and commission of Peter, would not permit him to deny his Saviour again.

Jesus asks: 'Simon do you love me?' It is easy for me to identify with that sentence – Simon is my name. I read it as if our Lord is addressing it directly to me. But we all need to put our name in the place of Simon – for Jesus addresses us too: 'John, do you love me? Anna, do you love me? Michael, do you love me? Francis, do you love me? Vanessa, do you love me? Will, do you love me? Amanda, do you love me? Andrea, do you love me? Justin, do you love me?' And worship is a life and a song and a gift that says and that shows 'Yes Lord, you know that I love you – not as much as you love me, but I do.'

Sometimes love grows cold. Jesus warned that this would be the mark of many in the last days – temptations and trials would cool their ardour for Christ. Jesus, in a message to the Ephesian church commended them for many things, but said he had one thing against them: 'You have forsaken the love you had at first.'* Even as some marriages grow cold, stale, dull – the way people sometimes lose their appetite and affection for each other's company – perhaps you have lost that love for God? Maybe you have allowed a moon to eclipse the love between you and Jesus – perhaps it is the demands of career, studies, relationships, family or hobbies. Maybe the pressures of life and the cares of this world have just caused that passion for Jesus to dissipate and turn your faith into religion, joy into duty? It is good to ask ourselves: 'Was there ever a time when Jesus was

* Revelation 2:4.

nearer and dearer to me? And if so, what happened?' Shakespeare's Othello said to Desdemona: 'when I love thee not – chaos is come again.'[132] When we love God, life is put in order. We are made to love God. It is in our DNA, it's our destiny. Only when we love God are we ourselves, fully alive, fully human. We find ourselves losing ourselves in loving Jesus.

## DO YOU KNOW JESUS LOVES YOU?

Our love is a response to Christ's love for us – our worship a response to the God who has graced us with worth. St John wrote, 'We love (Jesus) because he first loved us.'* Our love is response, it is second order – his love is *a priori*, the love of the one who knew us before we were formed. Truly, God's love takes the initiative. The Danish philosopher and prophet, Søren Kierkegaard wrote this prayer,

> 'You loved us first O God ... If I rise at dawn and in the very second of my awakening my soul turns to you in prayer, you have already beat me to it; You have already turned in love toward me.'[133]

> *Peter turned and saw that the disciple whom Jesus loved was following them. (This was the one who had leaned back against Jesus at the supper and had said, 'Lord, who is going to betray you?')*

JOHN 21:20

I confess I have often been troubled by this phrase 'The disciple whom Jesus loved' – which John uses of himself, to describe himself, six times in his Gospel. I felt that it implied a favouritism, that Jesus indeed had his golden boys, his preferred, chosen, select, 'in-crowd'. And I guess deep down I felt excluded from that inner core, on the outside, never quite making it in. And in this false sense of rejection, I also became somewhat resentful of those who seemed to be more 'in with the Lord' like John, the Beloved, who leant on the breast

* 1 John 4:19.

of Jesus. I readily identified with Peter, especially in his impetuous behaviour, zeal without wisdom, and bravado wed to failure. But John? Well John was the disciple I didn't connect to, either his depiction in the Gospels or his epistles. This resentment of the 'Beloved disciple' was really jealousy and insecurity – I reckoned that John was the sort to wear a t-shirt stating: 'Jesus loves you but I'm his favourite' – and I thought 'I'm sure he does, but does he love me?'

This deep sense of rejection affected my religion, my perception of others and of God. It affected my worship, my devotion. I unconsciously reasoned that if Jesus had favourites like John, special Beloveds, then maybe I could graduate to this inner core and be a beloved disciple. I knew I was justified by grace through faith ... but could I get promoted?

I wondered if perhaps by spending longer in my quiet times, perhaps by working harder at sharing my faith, perhaps by giving more than my tithe, such effort would impress the Lord and improve my ranking.

As a young minister, I once asked the milkman (yes, there was a time when men delivered milk to the door before breakfast) what time he started his work. He told me 4am. I reasoned that I worked for God, and I ought to be the first person at work in the town, not the milkman – and so used to get up at 3:30 – and spend the next five hours before breakfast, praying, studying and snoring. I wanted Jesus to take notice of me, and say 'Son, come up higher'. Not just the zeal of youth, it was a longing to feel like a Beloved disciple. If I prayed harder than others, studied harder than others, gave harder than others, worshipped harder than others, then maybe God would love me 'as much' as others.

If religion isn't grounded in being loved, it will be grounded in legalism. Many of us, not understanding that we are loved, strive and strain to gain favour. I simply failed to really understand that he loved me as much as he could, he had no more love to give, for he had already directed all of it to me at Calvary. Unless we know the Father's love, we tend toward the attitude of the older brother in the parable of the Prodigal Son[*] – we cannot enjoy the party, we resent the Father's grace to our brothers and sisters – we can even resent God: 'all these years I've slaved for you and you've never given me and my pals a goat', and we can't hear the Father crying 'my son, all I have is yours.'

Then, one day, when I was still a new chaplain in Oxford, I read John speaking of himself as 'the Beloved disciple' and I could feel the bile rising, the rejection, the resentments and then God spoke to me. Deep into my mind and spirit the words came: 'Simon, I don't love John any more than I love you. The only difference is that he knows he is loved.' I broke down into tears, deep wells opened up within me as God's love poured in and my rejection poured out. I knew it was true. Later Jesus expanded on the theme to me: 'On the night that I was betrayed John leant on my breast not because he was my favourite, but because he understood he was welcome – they all were, even Judas – but only he came and rested.' And we see that the first one leaning is the last one standing – the only one who entered into that intimacy with Jesus is the only one of the Twelve standing at Calvary.

John's self-given title, 'the Beloved disciple' was not arrogance, it was assurance. John didn't call himself 'the Beloved disciple' because he thought he was loved any more than others, but simply because he knew he was loved. His identity was secure in the affections of Christ. That day, the conservative in me wanted to test what I sensed God revealing to me. How do I know this is true? How do I know I too am a beloved disciple? The Lord immediately directed me to the Greek text of the book of 1 John, John the beloved's pastoral letter to the church. Six times, when addressing the believers, John uses the same title for them in the plural that he used of himself – they are *agapetoi*,

---

[*] Luke 15:11–32.

Deeply Beloved ones.* The NIV translates this as 'Dear Friends,' but that's just plain wrong, that would be the Greek word *philoi*. No, John is very clear: the description he uses for himself is the description he applies to the church – he, as we, are deeply beloved disciples. Even when, like Peter, we may only love Jesus with a lesser love, *philo*, he is always the *a priori* God who loves us with *agape*.

It is often said, but less often understood or believed, that God so loved the world that he gave his only begotten Son. We know the verses: 'greater love has no man than this than he lay down his life for his friend', and yet do we believe it? Listen, Jesus cannot love you any more than he already does – he has already loved us to death, his! Jesus is the only God the world ever heard of who loves sinners. The fourteenth century mystic, Catherine of Sienna, the only woman ever to be conferred the degree Doctor of Theology by the Catholic Church, often began her prayers addressing God, 'O Divine Madman'. When asked why she prayed this way, she replied that he is 'crazy with love, drunk with love'.[134]

How do we come to know this fierce love of God that pursues us relentlessly? Objectively, by meditating upon Calvary where publicly, concretely, geographically, unmistakably, he declares to heaven and hell and all in between that he is the God who loves us. Subjectively, by experiencing the witness of Spirit. For it is the Spirit who pours out the love of God into our hearts.** The Holy Spirit unites us to God's love. And as Paul wrote, knowing how desperately the church needs to experience this love of Christ in a knowing beyond knowing, Paul prays for us too, for more of the Spirit, that we may be: 'rooted and established in love' and 'grasp how wide and long and high and deep is the love of Christ, and to know this love that surpasses knowledge.'***

Do you know that Jesus loves you?

---

* 1 John 2:7; 3:2; 3:21; 4:1, 7, 11.
** Romans 5:5.
*** Ephesians 3:16–19.

Do you really know?

For years I 'believed' it – but it took too long to know it.

I have been inspired over the years by the ministry of Bible teacher and author Judson Cornwall. I once heard him tell the story of his brother Robert, who was pastor of a small church in Salem Oregon USA. He looked to supplement his struggling income as a counsellor at a local state psychiatric hospital. When he arrived they took him to Room 37. The sight that greeted Cornwall took his breath away. This was a padded room reserved for the most severe psychotic patients who walked around in a drug-induced daze, half naked, some in nappies, some just defecating on the floor. These people were no longer being treated, but, like caged animals, they were being controlled. This was many decades ago, before the sophisticated medical and psychiatric treatments of today. The Lord whispered to Cornwall: 'Sit on the floor.' Robert sat in the middle of filth. The Lord said: 'Sing a song.' From deep within he began singing, 'Yes Jesus loves me, yes Jesus loves me – the Bible tells me so'.

After an hour he was let out. A week later he returned to work and was taken back to Room 37! Again, he sang this song – this time a large black woman, touched deep in her being, drawn by love, sat behind him and joined in the song. He kept this up every visit. Within one month thirty-six of the patients had been transferred to self-help wards; and in less than a year all but two were released from the mental institution. In a year thirty-six had left hospital and two were members of his church. Oh, how the church needs to know God's love. That love which sets life in order. That love which expands our heart for God, fuels our passion for worship and fills our language of praise. Worship, true worship, is the adoring of the adored – the church of the Beloved, loving the Lover.[135]

Karl Barth was probably the greatest theologian since the Reformation – he published hundreds of books and articles, and his influence is clearly seen across the denominations and across the theological disciplines. Fifty years since his death it shows no sign of abating. On retiring in 1962, aged 76, Barth took a lecture tour of the USA. Speaking in Rockefeller Chapel, on the campus of the University of Chicago, during the Q & A time, a student asked Barth if he could summarize his whole life's work in theology in a sentence. Barth allegedly said something like, 'Yes, I can. In the words of a song I learned at my mother's knee: 'Jesus loves me, this I know, for the Bible tells me so'. This story appears in different guises, and has grown with the telling, embellished in detail by different preachers. Many have wondered if it was even true, but rather an urban myth, not least because some of the details and even location have changed.[136] It now seems clear he did say it, and not just the once.

# CHAPTER 17

# HE IS NOT THE *AU PAIR*

*And he is The Lord – he is God over us*

*There is not a square inch in the whole domain of our human existence over which Christ, who is Sovereign over all, does not cry: 'Mine!'*
ABRAHAM KUYPER

Jesus is not your *au pair*, home help, therapist or life coach. Jesus is not here to give your life a makeover. He is not a genie who emerges from a bottle when rubbed to dispense wishes. He is not your talisman. He is not your homeboy or your homie. He is not even your Rabbi. No. He is Christ, the Lord and God. Prince Charles holds numerous titles and honours. The most well-known is Prince of Wales and one day he will be King of England. Among the more unusual are Ojibway of Saskatchewan, which means 'The sun looks at him in a good way'; Colonel in Chief of the British Army; Air Commodore of the Royal Air Force; Admiral of the British Navy; Doctor of Letters; Doctor of Civil Law; Doctor of Music; Knight of the Order of the Bath; Knight of the Order of the Garter; Knight of the Order of the Elephant. All these names and titles are honorary and carry no executive power. Jesus Christ has several names and titles but his are not merely honorary – they convey all the executive power of the godhead. The Apostle Paul declared:

*Therefore God exalted him to the highest place*
*and gave him the name that is above every name,*
*that at the name of Jesus every knee should bow,*
*in heaven and on earth and under the earth,*

> *and every tongue acknowledge that Jesus Christ is Lord,*
>    *to the glory of God the Father.*

PHILIPPIANS 2:9–11

The pre-eminent predicate used of Jesus, more than any other, is Lord. This is the Greek word *kyrios* and has a range of meanings from 'master' to 'God'. However, in the Bible it primarily denotes divinity. In Old Testament Hebrew, God's ineffable name was *YAHWEH* (I am who I am). But devout Jews, not wanting to debase or defile this holy name on their sinful lips, substituted Yahweh for the name *Adonai*, or Lord. In the Greek version of the Old Testament, the Septuagint, the Hebrew name for God, *Adonai*, was translated as *Kyrios* – which means Lord, in the sense of 'God'. In the first century Jewish milieu to say *Kyrios* is to say God. And remarkably, this is what they called Jesus – over seven hundred times the Jewish authors of the New Testament, writing in Greek, use the name and title *Kyrios* for Jesus. These religious Jews knew the value of the words they used. There is no doubt that they were directly ascribing absolute divinity to him. And rightly so. Jesus Christ is God over all, forever praised.* And that makes it even more extraordinary that he who is Lord and God would stoop to be our friend, and brother, and Saviour.

## JESUS' LORDSHIP IS DEMONSTRATED

The Dutch theologian and prime minister, Abraham Kuyper famously stated 'there is not a square inch in the whole domain of our human existence over which Christ, who is Sovereign over all, does not cry: "Mine!"'[137]

- Jesus is Lord over *creation* – shoals of fish swam into nets at his nudge; he walked on water, and as the psalmist said,

---

* Romans 9:5.

*He stilled the storm to a whisper;*
*the waves of the sea were hushed.*

PSALM 107:29

- Jesus is Lord over *sickness*. He healed all who came to him – the deaf, the blind, the mute, the leper, the crippled – no disease was beyond his authority and compassionate power to transform.

- Jesus is Lord over the *demonic* – evil shadows that gripped personalities in their vile vice, he shattered and dispelled with a word – no demon could withstand his command.

- Jesus is Lord over the *spiritual* – Jesus asserted himself above Moses and even the *Torah*, claiming authority to interpret and inaugurate: again and again he said, 'You have heard that it was said … But I say unto you …'.* Jesus asserted himself above the sacred Sabbath: his disciples picked ears of corn on the Sabbath acting in an unlawful way and when Pharisees (perhaps understandably) rebuked them, Jesus said 'The Son of Man is Lord of the Sabbath'** – he is Lord of God's day! Jesus asserted himself over the temple. After his triumphant procession into Jerusalem, he strode into the temple courts and in a fury drove out the money changers and traders, as Malachi foresaw, 'Then suddenly the Lord you are seeking will come to his temple'. He went even further and claimed he *was* the temple and when destroyed would rise again in three days. No wonder the authorities accused him of blasphemy – if he wasn't the Lord he claimed to be, he was being blasphemous.*** The resurrection proved his assertion. Jesus is Lord.

---

* Matthew 5:21–22, 27–28, 31–34.
** Matthew 12:1–8.
*** Malachi 3:1; John 2:21.

- Jesus is Lord over *sin* – and he forgave all who looked to him – the tax collector, the woman caught in adultery, the crippled man lowered through the roof. The Pharisees balked at this, 'who can forgive sins but God alone?'* Indeed, no one but God.
- Jesus is Lord over *history* – Jesus was not victim of his situation and circumstance but Lord over time and history. Personalities and authorities all marched to his drum, fulfilling his decree, his destiny. The historian, HG Wells, in his book *The Outline of History*, wrote 'Is it any wonder that to this day this Galilean is too much for our small hearts.'[138]
- Jesus is Lord over *death* – Jesus had the power to reverse the very curse of Eden and bring life into death: he raised Lazarus, he raised the widow's son, he raised Jairus' daughter. Nothing withstood his power.**

Pre-eminently, it is his resurrection that vindicates his divine lordship. When Thomas, who doubted the witness of the other disciples and the empty tomb, saw for himself Jesus risen and glorious and victorious before him, he did the only thing appropriate, he fell at his feet in worship and declared 'My Lord and My God'.*** Jesus, conqueror of death is no longer 'Rabbi'.

Cosmic, spiritual, moral, natural, physical, historical, eternal – Jesus is sovereign Lord and King over all. In the classical world, the Greek god Atlas strained to hold up heavens, but Mother Julian had a beautiful vision of Jesus holding the world like an acorn in his hand. Yes – this is our Jesus.

* Mark 2:7.
** John 11:1–44; Luke 7:11–17; Mark 5:21–43.
*** John 20:24–29.

## JESUS' LORDSHIP IS CONTESTED

The demonic has always wanted to hold Jesus' title and wield his power. There have always been pretenders and usurpers to the King's throne. Satan sought to sit on Jesus' throne but was hurled from heaven. The great dragon fought against God for supremacy in heaven. The evil serpent fought for control of Adam and Eve in the garden; Baal and Asherah fought to supplant Yahweh from Israel's hearts. At Jesus' birth, when the Magi declared their desire to worship the King of the Jews, the puppet King Herod murdered infants to maintain his power. Satan sought to buy Jesus off by offering him all the wealth of the world if only Jesus would bow and worship him. In Jerusalem the Jewish elite manipulated Roman consul Pilate to have Jesus executed so as to maintain the balance of their power.[*] Emperor Nero gave himself the title 'the Lord of the Whole Earth' and put to death those Christians who recognized no other Lord but Jesus. Successive Roman emperors demanded all citizens sacrifice to them and hail them as Lord – and again, when Christians refused, they were fed to the lions.

'Jesus is Lord' is a profoundly political statement – it sends shock waves through every other authority and claims their submission. No wonder Islamism, Communism, Nazism, Secularism all have refused to recognize the lordship of Jesus and have sought through threat and terror to suppress and supplant the lordship of Jesus over his church. In 1934 the Swiss theologian Karl Barth refused to sign an unqualified oath to Hitler required of all university professors; he also refused to say 'Heil Hitler' or sing the German national anthem at the start of each lecture. Instead, he asked his students to sing a Christian hymn and say the Lord's Prayer. He was soon kicked out of the country, being Swiss. Had he been German he would have been executed in Sachsenhausen with many other brave and

---

[*] Isaiah 14:13; Revelation 12:7–9; Genesis 3; Judges 6; Matthew 2; Matthew 4:1–11; Matthew 27.

faithful Christians. Barth supported the Confessing Church, which was made up of those pastors faithful to Christ who refused to do homage to Hitler. Most German ministers drank the Kool Aid and were by their silence and acquiescence complicit to the greatest evil of the twentieth century. Barth penned the famous Christian political statement, the Barmen Declaration, making clear the church's relationship to the State when the state wanted to control the church:

> We reject the false doctrine that there could be areas of our life in which we would not belong to Jesus Christ but to other lords, areas in which we would not need justification and sanctification through him.[139]

Today, in the West, we live with the tyranny of Relativism. Absolute moral or spiritual truth claims are anathema and the only absolute allowed is not to be absolute. It is the very absoluteness of the lordship of Christ that is so provocative, so offensive, and which precipitates a crisis.

It was precisely the absolute truth of God and the absolute claim of Jesus as One Lord, rejecting the polytheism of the Romans, that brought the wrath of Rome down on the early church. The Pantheon in Rome is a magnificent circular structure built in 27BC and reconstructed in AD120. Its purpose was to unite the conquered peoples of the empire by providing a central place for all their gods. When the Christians were offered a niche for a statue of Jesus they refused, saying that Jesus could never stand beside other gods which are no gods. In AD609 the pantheon became an exclusively Christian church. In the nineteenth century, a British archaeologist investigating the ruins discovered that every chamber that once held an idol statue was now empty, except for one in which was a statue of Jesus.

Despite the tyranny of persecution in many different parts of the world, including imprisonment, execution and even beheading – in countries like North Korea, Iran, Nepal, Syria, in Pakistan and in

Communist China – tens of thousands are converted to Jesus each day. In February 2015, ISIS beheaded twenty-one migrant workers, all Coptic Christians. Given the chance to embrace Islam and live, they refused. They chose eternal life. On their knees, moments before their heads were severed, they prayed 'Jesus is Lord'. Christians are the most persecuted religious group in the world,[140] and yet the church is growing. The whole earth will be filled with knowledge of glory of the Lord Jesus.

## JESUS' LORDSHIP IS CONSUMMATED

Many now recognize Jesus for who he is, Lord. The Father knows, the angels know, the demons know, those who have met him know. Some see and accept him, whilst many reject him. Mary, pregnant with Jesus, was greeted by Elizabeth saying, 'And why is this granted to me that the mother of my Lord should come to me?'* She recognized that even *in utero*, as a fetus, Jesus was Lord of all. The letter to the Hebrews says, 'Now in putting everything in subjection to him, he left nothing outside his control. At present, we do not yet see everything in subjection to him.'** At present, no, but the day is set, and racing towards us when Jesus' lordship will be extended and acknowledged over all. On that day God will 'highly exalt him' before the whole universe and he whom the world once dismissed, scorned, and crucified, and who has been rejected and despised among men, on him God will publicly confer the name that is above every name and at that name every knee will bow and every tongue confess he is Lord. The Father is not making the Son the Lord, he is disclosing it for all to see. A thousand years before Christ's birth, King David had the same vision of Jesus:

* Luke 1:43 (ESV).
** Hebrews 2:8 (ESV).

*The LORD says to my lord*
*'Sit at my right hand*
*until I make your enemies*
*a footstool for your feet.'*

PSALM 110:1

*Every knee will bow* before Jesus as Lord. Every person who has ever
lived, high born and low, pre-historic and post-modern, male and
female, good and bad, all, myriad upon myriad for mile upon mile,
will be brought before Jesus and will bow their knees before him,
recognizing him as Lord. I like to think it will be every creature
too, everything with knees will bow – elephants with their two back
knees, birds and bees with their knees, even spiders with their 48
knees. Just imagine it, all creation bowing and acknowledging the
Lord. In 2005 a CT scan showed that the mummified Egyptian
Pharaoh Tutankhamun suffered a severe break in the bone above
his left knee that some scholars claim became infected and led to his
death.[141] He should have bowed the knee to the God of the Hebrews.
Many have infected knees and won't bow now – but one day they
will be made to kneel. Those who have refused to bow the knee to
Jesus as Lord in this life, will remain on their knees for eternity. And
to those who knelt freely in this life, Jesus will say,

'Arise my darling;
my beautiful one, come with me'*

## JESUS' LORDSHIP APPROPRIATED

The Apostle Paul said,

*If we live, we live for the Lord; and if we die, we die for the Lord. So,*
*whether we live or die, we belong to the Lord.*

ROMANS 14:8

* Song of Songs 2:10.

178

A Christian is one who gives total allegiance to Christ as Lord. A Christian lives a Jesus-centered life; Jesus is governor, king, master and head. That Jesus is Lord means he sets the terms and his wish is our command. Jesus said, 'why do you call me "Lord, Lord" and not do what I say?'* Our life is not our own; to say 'Jesus is Lord' is to relinquish all rights. Yet many people want Jesus as Saviour, but don't want Jesus as Lord. We want saving but we want to remain in control. Jesus is Lord means he cannot be a veneer to an otherwise secular life. Jesus is not your *au pair*, home help, personal therapist, life coach or hobby. The pastor and prophet Dietrich Bonhoeffer, who was murdered for opposing Hitler, put it this way,

> He did not go to the cross to ornament and embellish our life. If we wish to have him, then he demands the right to say something decisive about our entire life.[142]

Let me highlight three areas we find it so difficult for him to be Lord of.

*Lord of our money*: a few years ago, a Barna report concluded that seventy-two percent of Americans believed that God blesses people so that they can enjoy life as much as possible; fifty-eight percent agreed with the proposition that the primary purpose of life is enjoyment and fulfillment. Ronald Sider writes: 'As we got richer and richer, evangelicals chose to spend more and more on themselves and give a smaller and smaller percentage to the church. Today, on average, evangelicals in the USA give about two-fifths of a tithe. In 2002, Barna discovered that only six percent of born-again adults tithed – a fifty percent decline from 2000, when twelve percent did. And in 2002, just nine percent of Barna's narrow class of evangelicals tithed.'[143] The wallet is the hardest thing to get converted.

*Lord of our Relationships.* I don't want to tread heavily but many are simply not willing to follow the Bible's instructions on sex and relationships. I take a traditional position, and I believe the Bible

---

* Luke 6:46.

is clear: for the Christian, a permanent, exclusive, heterosexual marriage to another Christian is God's ordained locus for sexual intimacy. We must ask ourselves, does my lifestyle and my relationships honour Jesus and his word? I know this is a deeply painful and sacrificial issue for some, but what does Jesus is Lord mean if he is excluded here?

*Lord of our Career.* James challenged those who say I'll go to this city or that and make money when they ought to say 'If it is the Lord's will'. Jesus cannot be Lord and excluded from your work. Are you doing what he wants where he wants as he wants? On one occasion Jesus called a man to be his disciple, but the man replied, 'first let me go and bury my father'.* How often do we profess Jesus as Lord and yet follow half-heartedly – saying 'yes, but first'. Jesus said, 'no buts, me first'.

Missionary, Jim Elliot, martyred by Aucan Indians in the 1950s, wrote in his journal 'Take my life – have it all, have it all'.[144] There is an old saying 'if Jesus is not Lord of all he is not Lord at all'.

In New Zealand a few years ago I met the remarkable missionary theologian Dr Mick Duncan. Mick had grown up in an abusive home. His mother walked out on the family when he was a boy and left a letter on his bed which he found when he came home from school! He became a hippy in the 1970s and was expelled from college after writing his exams while high on LSD – the content of which were not inspired and did not reach the required standard. He lived homeless for years on the streets, a drug user and dealer, so stoned he has no memory of two years of his life as the drugs have permanently erased the record on his brain. Occasionally he meets people who met or knew him then and they fill in the details. Amazingly, on the streets Mick met a Christian who cared for him and gave him a room and possessions and clothes and met all his practical needs. In the room loaned to him was a Bible on the coffee

* James 4:15 (ESV); Luke 9:59.

table. Mick began reading the Bible and fell in love with Jesus but understood and was challenged by the cost of following him. For nine whole months he wrestled with the decision of whether to follow Jesus or not, walking daily round Hagley Park Christchurch. He knew that Jesus was not there just for a life makeover, he had to be Lord of all or not Lord at all. Finally, in 1976, Mick says,

> In that room given to me, I got down on my knees and said to King Jesus 'I now pledge my troth, my loyalty to the King and my life will now be governed by an obedience that will come before all other obediences, there will now occur an allegiance shift, in the very core of my being, and that no matter what it costs, my life will be governed by a leader.' I began by saying Jesus is to be Lord, he's not just there to give us a lifeover. But when we make him Lord, he is the making of us.[145]

Mick, this crazed homeless drug dealer understood what it meant to follow Jesus, and to make Jesus Lord. And Jesus took Mick and made him a husband and father and missionary and professor, one who has travelled the globe compelling people to make Jesus Lord.

What would it take to make him Lord?

# CHAPTER 18

# HE IS COMING BACK

*And he is coming back to be with us*
*And he will judge the living and the dead*

*'But about that day or hour no one knows, not even the angels in heaven, nor the Son, but only the Father.'*
MATTHEW 24:36

History is not cyclical. It is not going around and round repeating itself over and over. The Bible teaches that history is linear, racing inexorably to a fixed point, a climactic, dramatic, emphatic and glorious goal: and that is the returning of our Lord Jesus and the bringing of his kingdom reign forever, God's kingdom come. The Lord Jesus is coming back. He's bringing down the curtain of our history as we know it, and he's drawing open the curtains on the glory of eternity.

History will end not in a manmade environmental catastrophe – not that that abdicates our responsibility to look after creation; on the contrary, knowing that he's going to recreate it we are to echo something of the future now, as well as exercising our responsibility as stewards. But the world will not bring itself to an end as a result of human failing. God won't allow that because he is in control. Thermonuclear exchange is not going to bring the world to an end – nevertheless, we must work and pray for peace among the nations. And the world won't come to an end through a form of cosmic mechanical inertia causing the world and the planets to just stop spinning – God is in control and things will end when he says so, according to his eternal purposes, his plan and his decree and his ultimate action, centred on the Lord Jesus.

One day as we are just going about our business, suddenly our ears will fill with the sound of trumpets, and the heavens will open, and myriad on myriad of angels will fill the skies, and the Lord will come, and he will gather his church and we will meet him in the air, and the dead in Christ will rise and meet Jesus in the air, and will be brought to Jerusalem from the four corners of the globe, and there heaven will join earth, there he will judge the living and the dead, and all will bow before the Lord of the universe, and there he will recreate the heavens and the earth. We will enter into an eternity of bliss and perfection and glory.

What a day that will be! The day of days. The day to end all days.

## HE WILL COME AGAIN TO JUDGE THE LIVING AND THE DEAD.[146]

These words have been the heartbeat across the church, across the nations, across the centuries. They are the great hope of the church – that Jesus is coming back and will put all things right. He is not only our personal Lord, but Lord of all, and as Lord will come again to rule.

The ancient church was deeply centered on the return of Jesus and his judgment. The Apostles wrote about it – in the 216 chapters of the New Testament there are 318 references to Jesus' second coming, one for every thirty verses. Twenty-three of the twenty-seven New Testament books refer to it; there are eight times more references in the New Testament to Christ's second coming than there are in the Old Testament to his first. It was the focus of the apostolic preaching of the church and her sacraments. Whenever they met, they took the sacrament and proclaimed the Lord's death, looking backwards, to the cross, and looking forwards to his coming again. It was the hope of the church in the midst of persecution, and always has been, she was buoyed and strengthened by the hope that the Lord will return and end suffering and bless her and bring judgment on those who persecute her. It was the incentive for holy living. It was heralded in her creeds; it was painted on her wall friezes and ceilings. Ancient Jewish people greeted one another with *Shalom*, or 'Peace' or 'Wholeness', but the first early Jewish Christians quickly changed this to 'Maranatha – O Lord Come'.

But some in the church today are rather confused about the return of Jesus. In a 2013 survey by the US Fact Tank, The Pew Center on Religion and Public Life, only 27% believed the statement 'Jesus will definitely return' while 10% believed 'Jesus definitely will not return'; 20% Jesus *probably will* return; 28% *Jesus probably will not return*. Such statistics are surprising, indeed, bizarre, in a country where 75% claim to be Christian. Only 37% have some hope in Jesus' return and half those who claim to be Christians don't believe a core Christian belief. It is ironic that the Pew Center research also found that half of all Muslims in the world believe Jesus will return in their lifetime.[147]

The Bible speaks of his return as his 'revealing' – the Greek word is *apocalypsis** from which we get our term apocalypse. This word in modern idiom often conjures the image of cataclysm, disaster, destruction, the end of the world, ecological catastrophe, anarchy and even zombies. Certainly, before the end the demonic will do as much damage as he can before the Lord calls time and the trumpets sound. But the theme of apocalypse in the Bible centres on Jesus' return – it is pre-eminently his apocalypse, his unveiling, his revealing, his manifesting. The first time Jesus came he was incognito, God in humility and dependency enfleshed in a dark womb. But the next time Jesus comes, he will be unmissable and visible to all, in blazing divinity, majesty and glory: 'God without disguise, something so overwhelming that it will strike either

---

* 2 Thessalonians 1:7.

irresistible love or irresistible horror into every creature. It will be too late then to choose your side,' as CS Lewis saw.[148]

The first time Jesus came, the only witnesses were a few local shepherds and wise men from the East, plus some animals who shared their stable with the Holy Family. The next time there will be no missing him, no mistaking him, every eye will see, and every tongue confess Jesus is Lord. I don't know how that will happen, but it is not hyperbole. In 1969 over 500 million watched the Apollo 11 moon landing live; in 1985 1.9 billion apparently watched Live Aid, which, if accurate, meant 40% of the world's population at the time watched that concert; in 2018 1.9 billion tuned in to watch the wedding of Meghan Markle and Prince Harry. But the whole world will spectate this spectacular return of Jesus for his church. And they will not only spectate, but participate, for all will see and all will bow.

He is coming back. Are we ready?

There is great mystery over the details of his returning – we have the big brush strokes but not so much fine detail. God keeps his own counsel – and much of what will occur is so far outside our experience that we have nothing in our lives to frame it, neither language not conception for it; we just don't have an experience to compare it to. We don't have all the jigsaw pieces, and we don't have the picture, of what the end time will look like.

But we have enough to be certain of this hope: Jesus will come back, Jesus will pay back, and Jesus will put back.

## JESUS WILL COME BACK

### WHEN WILL HE RETURN?

When? Only God knows. Many have presumed to posit various different dates – it is amazing how many have had a go, and most of those dates have come and gone and so they were wrong. Bizarrely, some have stood by those dates and said he came incognito. I think not. Jesus said 'only the Father knows' the day or the hour he has set.[*] Of course, I suspect Jesus now knows. However, Jesus did say that even though we don't know the date or time, we might know the season. He said that just as we can look at the leaves on a tree and know it is winter or spring, summer or autumn, similarly we need to observe in the natural signs that indicate Jesus' coming draws closer. This will give us indicators as to where we are at on that line, on that trajectory, moving ever nearer toward the return of our Lord. And there are lots of signs that the Lord Jesus himself, particularly in Matthew 24, highlights. And the church has identified several key texts believed to give detail on the season of the end times, including: Daniel 12; Zechariah 12–14; Matthew 24; 2 Timothy 3:1–5; 2 Peter 3:3; and Revelation 13.

Now, many of the signs drawn from these texts have always been seen in history. It is my belief that we will see a concentration and clustering of these features as Jesus draws near. As we approach the end.

- Jesus talks about international disaster: there will be wars and rumours of war, with nation rising against nation. The world will not become more peaceful – politics cannot exorcise the sin of Cain. We've always seen that, but it will become more prominent, more significant.
- There will be ecological disaster: there will be earthquakes, famines and ecological disaster, perhaps the result of human exploitation and global warming. Revelation tells us that a third of the water will be undrinkable, it will be bitter.
- There will be cosmological disaster: the atmosphere will be severely polluted, causing the moon to change colour and stars will be falling to the ground and bringing destruction.
- There will be moral collapse: there will be an increase of wickedness, the rise of the 'man of lawlessness', a kind of

[*] Matthew 24:36.

personification of evil that will ape the kingdom of Christ, a false Messiah.

- There will be a political disaster: a rise of this anti-Christ figure, evil personified, a puppet played by the evil one appearing to offer peace to a world in crisis, offering 'peace, peace where there is no peace',* and for a while the world will be deceived and they will all back him, and then trouble will come, and he will rule with an iron rod and bring suffering. One of the marks of Revelation 13, if you read it like I do, is it will look like a one world economic and political and religious system that will seek to be imposed.
- Ecclesiastical disaster: the church will suffer a great tribulation, and the persecution of the church will bring the great apostasy.

There will be two positive signs of the impending return of Jesus: the Gospel will go to the nations and the Jews will return to their land from the nations. But this latter will incur the wrath of the demonic and the nations will turn to destroy Israel – Israel will return to the land, the nations will turn on Israel in rage, and this will intensify, and Israel will turn *en masse* to Jesus and then Jesus will return.

These are accelerating – Jesus' return is nearer now than it's ever been.

## HOW WILL HE RETURN?

Jesus will come differently. We will see a side of Jesus we haven't seen before: and what a wonderful side it will be. His first coming was as a meek and gentle Lamb, his second coming will be as a roaring Lion. The first coming he lay vulnerable in a manger, at his second coming he will sit omnipotent on heaven's throne; at his first coming Jesus did come incognito, ignored by most, seen only by the very few,

---

* Jeremiah 6:14.

those who had eyes to see; at his second coming every eye will see and every tongue confess that he is Lord; at his first coming many sat in judgment on him, at his second coming he will judge the world.

Jesus will come personally. He will come himself, as himself, personally and physically. He's not coming as a hologram. This will not be a 'spiritual' ethereal visit, as the false prophet Rudolf Steiner claimed. He is coming for his church, and the groom doesn't send his best man on his behalf to the wedding. The prophet Zechariah stated 'On that day his feet shall stand on the Mount of Olives'. Jesus took on human flesh in the incarnation, he remains the Word made flesh. Jesus rose physically, materially, corporeally – the tomb was empty of his body – in his body, transformed, immortal but not immaterial. Yes, bodily he met the disciples, and in body he ascended to heaven. There is a man seated in heaven and in that body he will return and as the Apostle John wrote, he is *coming* (present participle) in the flesh.*

And so, I believe this also implies Jesus will come geographically – given his physicality, he will come geographically, spatially. 'On that day his feet shall stand on the Mount of Olives that lies on the east of Jerusalem and the Mount of Olives shall be split in two, forming a great valley'. Zechariah prophesied, St John's apocalypse prophesied, the Angels prophesied his physical coming – and Jesus promised as much: 'Jerusalem, Jerusalem, you will not see me again until you say, "Blessed is he who comes in the name of the Lord."' They haven't said it yet. But that day will come, when they will see and will say. Jesus will triumphantly stride into Jerusalem, destroying Israel's enemies and there sit on the throne of David and from there the nations will be brought to be judged and to offer homage and from there he will reign over the new heaven and on earth.**

---

* Zechariah 14:4; 2 John 7.
** Zechariah 14:4; Matthew 23:39.

## JESUS WILL PAY BACK

'He will come again to judge the living and the dead' – the Creed here echoes the Apostle Peter, 'they will have to give an account to him who stands ready to judge the living and the dead.'* Twentieth century New Testament scholar Oscar Cullmann observed, 'Judgment is the primary eschatological function of the Son of Man.'[149]

People have always wanted to play God and put God in the dock. The Physicist Einstein was playing God when he confidently stated, 'I cannot imagine of a God who rewards and punishes his creatures...'[150] And again, 'I cannot conceive of a personal God who would directly influence the actions of individuals, or would directly sit in judgment on creatures of his own creation.'[151] I suspect 200,000 Japanese killed by two atomic bombs will welcome a day of judgment when a personal God will directly sit in judgment on him, the same man whose personal direct intervention in writing to the president of the USA helped kick start the Manhattan Project leading to the atomic bomb and the hell unleashed on Hiroshima. Einstein telling God what he can and cannot be and do is a strange thing, but not uncommon. People have always wanted to create God after their own image and impulses.

At his first coming people sat in judgment on Jesus. The Pharisees, the Sadducees, the crowd, Herod, Pilate, all the world have sat in judgment on him. But soon he will return and sit in judgment on them, on us. And what will matter then and forever after is not their judgment of him, but his of them. No longer 'gentle Jesus meek and mild', not the nursery book image of a shepherd carrying a lamb on his shoulders – but with the scales of justice in his hand and a sword in his mouth. TS Eliot got it right, 'in the juvescence of the year came Christ the tiger.'[152] Jesus is not Father Christmas, he is heaven's undefeated champion and conqueror of sin, death, and hell.

* 1 Peter 4:5.

Paul named this the day of wrath,* the Anglo-saxons called it *Domisday* – Doomsday. These are serious things. This is why we can't just live our lives centred on ourselves.

- Who is Jesus to judge? He is God and it's in his job description.
- Who will he judge? Everyone – the living and the dead.
- What will he judge? Everything – we have ever said, done and thought. Thank God for mercy.
- How will he judge? On the basis of his omniscience and perfect justice.
- Why will he judge? Because God is just, and a just judge must judge. He will judge because he cares – he will judge because justice must be done. He will judge because not to judge is to be somehow indifferent, because justice is not done in this life.

JI Packer, in his classic introduction to Christian thought *Knowing God*, writes: 'the character of God is the guarantee that all wrongs will be righted someday; when the day of God's wrath, when his righteous judgment will be revealed, retribution will be exact, and no problems of cosmic unfairness will remain to haunt us. God is the Judge, so justice will be done.'[153]

- Jesus will judge us based on his moral perfections and divine law.
- Jesus will judge us on whether we have loved God and our neighbour.
- Jesus will judge us on whether we have clothed the naked, fed the hungry, visited our brothers and sisters in prison.
- Jesus will judge every word we have spoken, every secret of our hearts.
- Jesus will judge us on whether we trusted in his death for our forgiveness.

* Romans 2:5.

- Jesus' judgment will be final, there is no court of appeal.

I did a parish mission in Portsmouth in 1988. The single men on the team camped down in sleeping bags in a church hall. On the first night, at about midnight, as we lay fast asleep, suddenly the church bells began to sound and a cacophony shattered our sleep and rudely shook us awake. The chap next to me sat bolt up in his bag, still half asleep, and shouted in sheer terror: 'I'm sorry, I'm sorry!' Then he came round and realized it was the church bells. He said to me 'I thought it was the second coming'. He later became a missionary to India. For we who love Jesus, we look up in eager anticipation, his return holds no terror for us. But for those who have dismissed Jesus as Lord, they will pray for the mountains to fall on them and hide them. William Dodd, an eighteenth-century Anglican clergyman, wrote a poem called 'Thought on the glorious epiphany of Jesus Christ'. One stanza begins 'Pardon Dread Lord' – that's all Jesus needs to hear,[154] and he will pardon.

## JESUS WILL PUT BACK

'Jesus will return just as he promised,' said the angels to the disciples who watched him ascend. 'I will come back to take you to be with me,' said Jesus, and he always keeps his word.* When he comes as the triumphant and glorious King, he will make all things right. All creation is groaning – and has been since the spiritual earthquake in Eden – awaiting the day of redemption when Jesus returns and restores all things. He will finally and fully rout his nemesis who will be thrown into the lake of fire and brimstone. All evil will be extinguished in fire. Toward the end of *The Lord of the Rings*, Samwise Gangee, totally overwhelmed by his pilgrimage to Mount Doom and the destruction of ring, has been in a very deep sleep. When he awakes, he thinks everything is lost, but soon discovers

---

* Acts 1:6–11.

instead that all his friends are with him – he cries out: 'Gandalf. I thought you were dead! But then I thought I was dead! Is everything sad going to come untrue?'[155] Yes, everything sad will come untrue when Jesus returns and makes all things right.

# HOW DO WE PREPARE FOR JESUS' RETURN?

## READINESS

Jesus himself told us, 'So you also must be ready, because the Son of Man will come at an hour when you do not expect him'.* Renowned preacher and author, G Campbell Morgan, would often say 'I never begin my work in the morning without thinking that perhaps he may interrupt my work and begin his own'. We should live our lives so that if he returned today, if he interrupted us, whatever we were doing, thinking, saying wouldn't cause us embarrassment or shame.

## STEADINESS

'You too be patient and stand firm, because the Lord's coming is near'; 'Here is a call for the endurance and faith of the saints'.** These suggest that amidst the end time tribulations, God won't rapture us out of trouble, instead he calls us to be steady, to stand firm in and through them. To endure not escape. The wonderful Corrie ten Boom, who survived being a Nazi prisoner in Belsen, once said:

> 'I have been in countries where the saints are already suffering terrible persecution. In China the Christians were told "don't worry, before tribulation comes, you will be translated, raptured." Then came a terrible persecution. Millions of Christians were tortured to death. Later I heard a Bishop from China say, sadly "We have failed. We should have made the people strong for persecution, rather than

* Matthew 24:44.
** James 5:8; Revelation 13:10 (ESV).

telling them Jesus would come first." Turning to me he said "Tell the people how to be strong in times of persecution, how to stand when tribulation comes – to stand and not to faint."[156]

## HOLINESS

What bride would ever walk down the aisle to meet her groom with hair unkempt, make-up and nails undone, teeth unbrushed, wearing her gardening clothes? Christ the lover is coming for his beloved. And knowing this, we must prepare ourselves. The Holy One comes for a holy bride. 'But we know that when Christ appears, we shall be like him ... all who have this hope in him purify themselves'.[*]

## JOYFULNESS

Not a grubby bride, nor a glum bride. Despite the tribulations and the trials, we ought to be filled with inexpressible joy, knowing our God, our Lover, our Groom draws near, he's coming to get us, to save us, the best is ahead. 'When these things begin to take place, stand up and lift up your heads, because your redemption is drawing near'.[**]

## WITNESS

When the disciples, before the ascension, asked 'are you at this time going to restore the kingdom to Israel?' Jesus replied that it was none of their business; their business was to wait and to receive power when the Spirit came upon them, and to be witnesses in Jerusalem, Judea and to the uttermost ends of the earth. Before the end time restoration of the kingdom to Israel under Messiah Jesus, they were to have gone to the ends of the earth witnessing! We know that in heaven's choir around the throne, there will be representatives from

[*] 1 John 3:2–3.
[**] Luke 21:28.

every tribe, tongue, people group, nation. For that to happen they must receive Christ. And so we must go, and make disciples of all nations, before Jesus returns. 'And the Gospel of the kingdom will be preached in the whole world as a testimony to all nations, and then the end will come.'*

## EXPRESS

Professor Stanley Grenz has written, 'Eschatology is a call to action in the present based on God's future.'[157] Yes. The vision of heaven leads us to activity not passivity. Blessed is the servant whose master finds him working when he returns. Our prayer and our labour must always be to see God's kingdom come on earth as it is in heaven. Glimpsing in part what heaven looks like – justice, righteousness, equality, unity, beauty, the nations together, creation not groaning - knowing in part what God wants and will bring we never just wait, but we work to see God's eternal will here in time.**

Again, we turn to CS Lewis for clarity on how we wait:

> … a continual looking forward to the eternal world is not … a form of escapism or wishful thinking, but one of the things a Christian is meant to do. It does not mean that we are to leave the present world as it is. If you read history you will find that the Christians who did most for the present world were just those who thought most of the next.[158]

## THE BEST TILL LAST

Samuel Rutherford, the great Scots Puritan who suffered imprisonment for his faith in an Aberdeen jail, from his cell had a ministry of letter writing which has brought great delight to the church for four centuries. In his final letter, days before he died, in March 1661:

*  Acts 1:8; Revelation 7:9; Matthew 24:14.
** 2 Peter 3:13–14.

Our royal kingly master is upon his journey, and will come, and will not tarry. ... It is possible that I shall not be an eyewitness to it in the flesh, but I believe he cometh quickly who will remove our darkness, and shine gloriously in the Isle of Britain, as a crowned king ... and this is the hope and confidence of a dying man who is longing and fainting for the salvation of God.[159]

When my son Nathanael was little, I used to cycle him to school and we would get to school and go into his class, and they had all their names on their pegs for their kit. And we got there, and he took off his kit bag and hung it up, and then took off his coat and hung it up, and hung up his woolly hat and then I would give him a kiss goodbye. One day I was in a real hurry to get to work, and as he began his routine – bag, coat, hat – I said 'Son, just give me a kiss, I've gotta go, I'm really busy I've got to get to work now!' And Nathanael looked at me and said, 'No! I save the best till last.'

And for we who say, 'Maranatha! Come Lord Jesus,' he saves the best till last. Jesus is saving the best till last. We who have accepted him in this life as Lord and Saviour have known his beautiful kindness to us, his love, his mercy, his forgiveness, his attentiveness, his power, his presence, his healing. He has changed our lives. He has made our lives. He has given us life. And he is coming for us, laden down with wedding gifts. He is glorious. He is coming for us. He is amazing.

The Bible closes with these words of Jesus: 'I am coming soon'[*] and the church responds, 'Amen. Come, Lord Jesus'. The grace of the Lord Jesus be with us all.

$$\dagger$$

[*] Revelation 22:20.

# HE KNOCKS AND HE WAITS

*Meanwhile he's still healing, still cleansing, still delivering, still inviting*

*'Here I am! I stand at the door and knock.'*
REVELATION 3:20

One of greatest British painters of the Victorian era was the Pre-Raphaelite artist Holman Hunt. My favourite work of his is called 'Scape Goat'. It depicts Jesus as the Lamb of God who takes away the sin of the world, with a red rag around its head, sent off into the wilderness to die there, cursed and carrying away our sin. I carried a postcard of this in my briefcase for over a decade, too crumpled and faded. But Hunt's most famous work is the English icon, 'Light of the World'. This was probably painted in the garden of Oxford University Press in the 1850s and was owned by an OUP printer, whose widow donated it to Keble College where it now hangs. It was based on the depiction of Jesus in John's Revelation, where Jesus says to the Church of Laodicea, 'Behold I stand at the door and knock.'* Hunt portrays beautiful Jesus, robed in splendour, standing outside a door, in a tangled garden, holding a lantern, wanting to come in. Hunt stated that he purposely did not paint a handle on the outside of the door, for only the individual inside can open the door of their heart. Jesus will never impose himself. He waits to be welcomed.

---

* Revelation 3:20 (ESV).

It is said the elderly Holman Hunt was upset when Keble College began charging people to see it, so he began another larger version, which was installed in St Paul's Cathedral in 1908 during a special service which included the reading from Revelation, 'Behold, I stand at the door and knock. If anyone hears my voice and opens the door, I will come in to him and eat with him, and he with me.' Many years later, the painting went to be cleaned from all the grime seeping into the Cathedral from traffic around St Paul's. When the restorer removed the frame and the moulding, there in script at the bottom, painted by the artist Hunt and to be seen by the Lord alone, was this prayer: 'Forgive me Lord Jesus that I kept you waiting so long.'[160]

Jesus is amazing. He stands at the door of our lives, and knocks, and knocks for he desires to come in and be with us. Don't keep him waiting. Open the door of your mind, your heart, your life, and say 'Please Jesus, come in'.

# ENDNOTES

1 *The Avengers* (Marvel Studios, 2012).

2 Brenda Myers-Powell, 'My 25 Years as a Prostitute' *BBC News Magazine,* 30 June 2015 bbc.co.uk (accessed November 2020).

3 Robert Cottrill, 'I Have Never Lost the Wonder of It All' *Wordwise Hymns,* https://wordwisehymns.com (17 February 2017).

4 Simon Ponsonby, *More: How You Can Have More of the Spirit When You Already Have Everything in Christ* (David C Cook, 2007).

5 Philip Yancey, 'The Encyclopedeia of Theological Ignorance' *Christianity Today,* 6 September 1999, p120.

6 Those words, preached the next Sunday, were put to music and image by some gifted creatives and joined by some photos to become a small gift book called *Amazing* (Muddy Pearl, 2019).

7 A beautiful line from Dietrich Bonhoeffer, *Letters and Papers from Prison,* ed. Eberhard Bethge (Simon & Schuster, 2011), p337. The word 'lees' in some translations is rendered as dregs.

8 Walter Isaacson, 'Einstein and Faith' *Time* (169) (5 April 2007), p47.

9 Charles Gabriel, 'My Saviour's Love' (1905).

10 Edward Pusey, *Sermons During the Season from Advent to Whitsuntide* (John Henry Parker, 1848), p64.

11 Donald Miller, *Blue Like Jazz* (Thomas Nelson, 2003), p233.

12 'How many people are homeless in the UK?' *The Big Issue,* 11 November 2020, bigissue.com (accessed November 2020).

13 To be precise, the winter solstice is generally on 21 December, although it can occur on 22 or even as early as 20 December. It marks the shortest day and the longest night of the year in the Northern Hemisphere.

14 Frederick Buechner, *The Longing for Home* (HarperSanFransisco, 1996), p7.

15 Pádraig Ó Tuama, *In the Shelter: Finding a Home in the World* (Hodder, 2015), p155.

16 Victoria Namkung '"I Loved God, I Loved Believing": an Interview with RO Kwon,' *Longreads* July 2018, Longreads.com (accessed November 2020).

17 Brent Landau 'Christmas from the Wise Men's Point of View: The Apocryphal Revelation of the Magi' Lecturing at Baylor Institute for Studies of Religion, 29 November 2017.

18 'How to Get Ready for Christmas,' amara.com.

19 'Miracle on Evergreen Terrace,' *The Simpsons*, Season 9, Episode 10 (Gracie Films and Twentieth Century Fox Studios, 21 December 1997).

20 Charles Morris, 'Christmas with Ann Voskamp: How in the World to Get Ready for Christmas?' *Haven Today,* 11 December 2013, haventoday.org.

21 Graham Stanton, *Jesus and Gospel* (Cambridge University Press, 2004).

22 Jo Brand, '100 funny jokes by 100 comedians' *The Telegraph*, 30 December 2017, thetelegraph.co.uk.

23 Suetonias, *Life of Vespasian*, 4.5.

24 JRR Tolkien, *The Silmarillion* (Harper Collins, 1999), p3.

25 Alfred Edersheim, *The Life and Times of Jesus the Messiah* (Hendrickson Publishers, 1993), p131.

26 Philo, 'Who is the heir of Divine Things', in *The Writings of Philo Judaeus of Alexandria Philo*, Book 17.

27 CS Lewis, *The Chronicles of Narnia: The Last Battle* (Bles, 1956), p132.

28 'Love came down at Christmas' is a line from a poem by Christina Rossetti initially published without title in *Time Flies: A Reading Diary* (1885).

29 Agnieszka Holland, *In Darkness* (Zebra Films, 2011). Original Polish title: *W ciemności*.

30 Shaye JD Cohen, 'The ways that parted: Jews, Christians, and Jewish-Christians ca. 100–150 CE', *Near Eastern Languages and Civilizations* (Harvard University, 2013), dash.harvard.edu.

31 Perhaps the best book on this is Susannah Heschel's *The Aryan Jesus: Christian Theologians and the Bible in Nazi Germany* (Princeton University Press, 2010).

32 Peter Stoner, *Science Speaks* (Moody Press, 1958).

33 Jonathan Bernis, *A Rabbi Looks at Jesus of Nazareth* (Chosen, 2011).

34 Mottel Baleston, imetmessiah.com, Ask Isaiah, youtube.com/watch?v=67fhPR-6YtRY.

35 Arnold Fruchtenbaum, 'The Genealogy of the Messiah', *Jews For Jesus,* 20 April 2018, jewsforjesus.org (accessed November 2020).

36 Howard Jacobson, 'Behold! The Jewish Jesus', *The Guardian*, 9 January 2009, theguardian.com.

37 Paula Fredriksen, 'Was Jesus Jewish? Why is it so important to us and why would it have coloured his perceptions?', *PBS Frontline*, 1998, pbs.org. See also: Paula Fredricksen, *From Jesus to Christ: The Origins of the New Testament Images of Jesus* (Yale Press, 1988).

38 Phyllis Stroh, 'The Jewish Messiah Miracle', Precious-Testimonies Website, precious-testimonies.com (accessed November 2020).

39 Mary Caroline Spalding, *The Middle English Charters of Christ*, p98, quod.lib. umich.edu.

40 *The Annotated Luther, Volume 2: Word and Faith*, ed. Kirsi I Stjerna (Fortress Press, 2015), p300.

41 Ruth Tucker, *Katie Luther, First Lady of the Reformation: The Unconventional Life of Katharina von Bora* (Zondervan, 2017).

42 Brian Douglas, *The Eucharistic Theology of Edward Bouverie Pusey: Sources, Context and Doctrine Within the Oxford Movement and Beyond* (Brill, 2015), p58.

43 Origen, 'Homilies on Luke 15:2' *The Fathers of the Church* (The Catholic University of America Press, 1996).

44 Dave Brannon, ed., *Our Daily Times with God* (Discovery House, 1988), p169.

45 John Keble, *Sermons for the Christian Year*, Vol 1, sermon 6, victorianweb.org.

46 Mary Black, 'Flesh and Blood,' *The Holy Ground* (1993).

47 Jim Irwin, *More Than Earthlings: An Astronaut's Thoughts for Christ-Centered Living* (Broadman Press, 1983).

48 Audra Czarnikow, 'God Walks the Dark Hills'.

49 Donda West and Karen Hunter, *Raising Kanye: life Lessons from the Mother of a Hip-Hop Superstar* (Simon & Schuster, 2007).

50 EM Bounds, *The Complete Works of EM Bounds on Prayer*, emboundsonprayer. wordpress.com.

51 John Wesley, *Life of the Rev. JW Fletcher, Vicar of Madeley*, abridged (Religious Tract Society, 1799), p25.

52 James Levine, quoted by Peta Bee, 'These feet were made for walking,' *The Guardian,* 27 March 2007, theguardian.com (accessed November 2020).

53 Søren Kierkegaard, 'Letter 150', *Letters and Documents*, vol 25 (Princeton, 2009), pxxii.

54 John Geiger, *The Third Man Factor: Surviving the Impossible* (Canongate Books, 2009), p42.

55 Kenneth Grahame, *The Wind in the Willows* (Egmont Books, 2003), p28–29.

56 Mark Helprin, 'River,' in *Freddy and Fredericka* (Penguin, 2006).

57 Henry David Thoreau, 1849 in *Walden, Civil Disobedience and Other Essays* (CreateSpace, 2016).

58 JRR Tolkein, Humphrey Carpenter, ed., *The Letters of JRR Tolkien* (Houghton Mifflin Harcourt, 2014).

59 The modern *Lutherbibel* has a footnote explaining that in 1524, Luther translated the Hebrew more faithfully: 'The 'strom' tide/flow/current with its brooks rejoices the city of God, the holy dwellings of the most high', but he altered this in 1531 to 'the city of God should remain very full of delight with its little fountains/springs, where the holy dwellings of the Most High are' – the river had dried up!

60 Charles Haddon Spurgeon, 'The indwelling and outflowing of the Holy Spirit' *Metropolitan Tabernacle Pulpit* Volume 28, spurgeon.org (accessed November 2020).

61 'Lost & found: Buried treasure is poised to reach a much wider audience' *Financial Times*, February 2018, *ft.com* (accessed 3 November 2020).

62 'Pembrokeshire chariot burial finds ruled as treasure' *BBC News,* 31 January 2019, bbc.co.uk (accessed 17 November 2020).

63 Thomas Aquinas, *Summa Theologicae: Latin text and English translation, introductions, notes, appendices, and glossaries,* tr. Thomas Gilbey (Cambridge University Press, 1964), II-II, question 35, article 4, reply 2.

64 Blaise Pascal, *Great Shorter Works of Blaise Pascal*, trs. Emile Caillet and John Blankenagel (Westminster Press, 1948).

65 CS Lewis, *Surprised by Joy: An accidental journey from atheism to Christianity* (Collins, 2012).

66 CS Lewis, *Letters to Malcolm: Chiefly on Prayer* (Mariner Books, 2007), p92–93.

67 John Piper, 'Thank you, Blaise Pascal,' *Desiring God*, 20 June 2011, desiringgod. org (accessed November 2020).

68 Dietrich Bonhoeffer, *The Cost of Discipleship*, tr. RH Fuller (SCM, 2015).

69 William Blake, *The Complete Poetry and Prose of William Blake*, ed. David Erdman (Anchor Books, 1988), p511.

70 JRR Tolkein, *Lord of the Rings* (Allen & Unwin, 1954).

71 Victor Frankl, *Man's Search for Meaning* (Beacon Press, 2006). Frankl is probably referring to 'Paradise Lost', and the full quotation is: 'For the first time in my life I was able to understand the meaning of the words, 'The angels are lost in perpetual contemplation of an infinite glory.''

72 CS Lewis, *Till We Have Faces* (Harper, 2017), pp75–6.

73 Jamie Snyder, *Like Jesus: Shattering our False Images of the Real Christ* (David C Cook, 2016).

74 Richard Sibbes, *The Bruised Reed and a Description of Christ* (Bibliotech Press, 2019).

75 Plato, quoted in Wynand de Beer, *Reality: From Metaphysics to Metapolitics* (Resource Publications, 2019), p212.

76 Ridley Scott, *Gladiator* (2000).

77 William Shakespeare, *Richard II* (Wordsworth Classics, 2015), Act 3, Scene 2.

78 'At a poker table, King Farouk was heard to remark: "Soon, there will be only five kings in the world, the four kings in a pack of cards and the King of England.' He was a bad king, but a good prophet.' Sasson Somekh, *Mongrels or Marvels: the Levantine Writings of Jacqueline Shohet Kahanoff*, ed Deborah A Starr (Stanford University Press, 2011).

79 Strider, 'The Fellowship of the Ring' (dir. Peter Jackson, 2001).

80 Fyodor Dostoevsky, 'Letter To Madame. ND Fonvisin (1854),' in *Letters of Fyodor Michailovitch Dostoevsky to his Family and Friends*, tr. Ethel Colburn Mayne (Macmillan, 1914), Letter XXI, p71.

81 'No One Cares About You – And That's Great,' *Forbes Magazine*, 26 March 2013, forbes.com.

82 CS Lewis, *Mere Christianity* (Geoffrey Bles, 1952), p55.

83 His story is told wonderfully in this video – he talks about Jesus as God around 36 mins in – well worth listening to it all: youtube.com/watch?v=HcwhIot-4W7o&feature=youtu.be.

84 Dante Alighieri, *The Divine Comedy* (Classics of World Literature: Wordsworth Edition, 2009).

85 JRR Tolkien, in Humphrey Carpenter, ed., *The Letters of JRR Tolkien* (Houghton Mifflin, 2000), p110. The letter to his son was written 30 January 1945.

86 William Shakespeare, *Macbeth*, Act 5, Scene 5.

87 St Augustine, quoted in Anthony C Thiselton, *The Hermeneutics of Doctrine* (Eerdmans, 2007), p519.

88 The Church of England *Articles*, churchofengland.org.

89 The Church of England, 'Holy Communion Service Order One' *Common Worship*, churchofengland.org.

90 George Herbert, 'The Holy Communion,' in *The Temple* (Penguin, 2017).

91 Richard Wurmbrand, 'The Beauty of Nothing,' sermon 9 March 2014, www.youtube.com/watch?v=iYG9HLR8iYc.

92 Oscar Wilde quoted in Russell Jackson, Ian Small and Joseph Bristow, eds., *The Complete Works of Oscar Wilde* (Oxford University Press, 2007), p119.

93 Julian of Norwich, *A Revelation of Love* (Gracewing, 2004), p25.

94 Charles Spurgeon, *Until He Comes: Twenty Reflections on the Lord's Supper* (Whitaker House, 2018).

95 The Church of England, 'Holy Communion Service Order One,' *Common Worship*, churchofengland.org.

96 The Church of England, 'The Apostles' Creed', churchofengland.org.

97 Paul Tillich, *The New Being* (University of Nebraska Press, 2005), p72.

98 Tertullian, *Anti-Nicene Fathers*, Volume III, De Corona (Of the crown) 3.4, tertullian.org.

99 Kevin Butcher, 'The Strange Afterlife of Pontius Pilate,' *History Today*, 25 March 2016, historytoday.com.

100 CS Lewis, *The Lion, the Witch and the Wardrobe* (Puffin Books, 1959), p139.

101 Cicero, quoted in John Stott, *The Cross of Christ* (IVP, 2006), p30.

102 William Edwards, Wesley Gabel and Floyd Hosmer, 'On the Physical Death of Jesus Christ,' *The Journal of the American Medical Association* (April 1986), researchgate.net.

103 Friedrich Nietzsche, *The Antichrist in Twilight of the Idols* and *The Anti-Christ* (Penguin, 1990), p62.

104 Rabbi Simcha Backman, 'Madonna: An Immaterial Girl?,' *Los Angeles Times*, 26 August 2006, latimes.com.

105 Richard Dawkins on Twitter (4 September 2012), https://twitter.com/richard-dawkins.

106 'The Harrowing of Hell' in *A Dictionary of Biblical Tradition in English Literature*, ed. David Lyle Jeffrey (Eerdmans, 1992), p332.

107 From a published sermon 'Saved by Grace' in Karl Barth, *Deliverance to the Captives* (SCM, 1961), pp35–42.

108 The Latin *Ecce Homo* from the Vulgate translation renders the Greek, where clearly Pilate was addressing the crowd and calling them to look at Jesus. The Latin *Ecce Homo* here is nominative – however in the vocative, addressing Jesus, 'Man, look' it would still be *Ecce Homo*.

109 Janssens, Titian, Caravaggio, Solario, Massys, Cerezo, Cigoli, De Champaigne, Chmielowski, Munkacsy, Wallinger.

110 'Spanish Fresco Restoration Botched By Amateur,' *BBC News*, 23 August 2012, bbc.co.uk.

111 Doreen Carvajal, 'A Town, if Not a Painting, Is Restored,' *New York Times*, 14 December 2012, nytimes.com.

112 I was inspired one morning in prayer to consider this thought. I later found a book written on this theme, with great attention to detail and beauty, written by a Catholic priest who lived in Jerusalem in the early twentieth century: republished now: AG Sertilllanges, *What Jesus saw from the Cross* (Sophia Institute Press, 1999).

113 Ron Warren, 'The Unique Tamid Sacrifice,' *Torah Life Ministry*, April 2010, torahlifeministry.com.

114 John Donne, 'Riding Westward,' Good Friday 1613.

115 Mary Poppins (dir. Robert Stevenson, 1964).

116 James S Stewart, *Heralds of God* (Charles Scribner and Sons, 1946), p15.

117 Phil Anderson, *Lord of the Ring: A Journey in Search of Count Zinzendorf* (Muddy Pearl, 2020), pp31–32. Some sources attribute this painting to Domenica Feti, others to Sternberg. The image can be viewed at zinzendorf.com.

118 Howard Carter, *The Tomb of Tut-ankh-amen: Discovered by the Late Earl of Carnarvon and Howard Carter* (Cambridge University Press, 2010).

119 Tony Campolo, *It's Friday, but Sunday's Comin'* (Thomas Nelson, 2008).

120 JRR Tolkein, *The Lord of the Rings* (HarperCollins, 2007), p104.

121 Archbishop Thomas Cranmer, 'The Order for Holy Communion' in *The Book of Common Prayer (1662, 1928)*, (OUP, 1928).

122 *The Complete Poems of Philip Larkin*, ed. Archie Burnett, Faber & Faber, 2014.

123 Ernest Becker, *The Denial of Death* (Free Press, 1997).

124 CS Lewis, *Miracles: A Preliminary Study* (Touchstone, 1996), p190.

125 David Watson, *Fear No Evil* (Hodder Christian paperbacks, 1984), p167.

126 Eugene Peterson, *Living the Resurrection: The Risen Christ in Everyday Life* (Nav Press, 2006), p14.

127 CS Lewis, ibid.

128 Leon Morris, *The Gospel of John* (NICNT, 1995), p772.

129 Elmer L Towns and Vernon M Whaley, *Worship Through the Ages: How the Great Awakenings Shape Evangelical Worship* (B&H Publishing Group, 2012), p211.

130 Ponsonby and Bennetts, *Now to Him*, (Monarch, 2006) p103.

131 Albert Camus, *The Plague*, tr. Stuart Gilbert (Vintage, 1991), p228.

132 William Shakespeare, *Othello*, Act 3 Scene 3.

133 Søren Kierkegaard in *Søren Kierkegaard: The Mystique of Prayer and Pray-er*, ed. George K Bowers (CSS, 1995), p27.

134 Ponsonby and Bennetts, ibid., p108.

135 Judson Cornwall and Michael Reid, *Whose Love Is It Anyway?* (Sharon Publications, 1991), pp58–59.

136 Roger E Olson, 'Did Karl Barth Really Say "Jesus Loves Me, This I Know…,"' *Patheos*, 24 January 2013, patheos.com.

137 Abraham Kuyper, 'Sphere Sovereignty,' in *Abraham Kuyper: A Centennial Reader*, ed. James D Bratt (Eerdmans, 1998), p488.

138 HG Wells, *Outline of History* (Jazzybee Verlag, 2013), p237.

139 Karl Barth, 'The Barmen Declaration,' from *Kairos: Three Prophetic Challenges to the Church*, ed. Robert McAfee Brown (Eerdmans, 1990).

140 Jennifer Wishon, Global Persecution Report, *CBN*, 22 September 2019, cbnnews.com.

141 Stephan Lovgren, 'King Tut Died from Broken Leg,' *National Geographic*, 1 December 2006, news.nationalgeographic.com (accessed November 2020).

142 Dietrich Bonhoeffer, 'Jesus Christ and the Essence of Christianity' in Geffrey Kelly and Burton Nelson, eds., *A Testament to Freedom: The Essential Writing of Dietrich Bonhoeffer* (HarperOne, 1995), p51.

143 Ronald J Sider, 'The Scandal of the Evangelical Conscience,' *Christianity Today*, February 2005, christianitytoday.com (accessed November 2020).

144 Jim Elliot, in *Jim Elliot*, ed. Susan Martins Miller (Barbour Publishing, 2004), p34.

145 Mick Duncan, speaking at a mission festival held in Long Gully, Bendigo, 2012, hosted by Seeds Bendigo and Cornerstone Community: vimeo.com/45049349 (accessed November 2020).

146 The Church of England, 'The Apostles' Creed,' churchofengland.org.

147 The full statistics can be viewed at Pew Research Center, 'Spring 2013 Survey,' *Pew Center on Religion and Public Life*, 1 May 2013, pewresearch.org (accessed November 2020).

148 CS Lewis, *Mere Christianity* (Macmillan, 1952), p51.

149 Oscar Cullmann, *God Is For Us*, ed. Simon Ponsonby (Monarch, 2013), p121.

150 Albert Einstein, *The World As I See It* (The Citadel Press, 1999), p5.

151 Albert Einstein, *The Human Side*, eds Helen Dukas and Banesh Hoffman (Princeton Press, 1976), p66.

152 TS Eliot, 'Gerontion,' in *TS Eliot, Collected Poems 1909-1962* (Faber & Faber, 1970).

153 JI Packer, *Knowing God* (Hodder & Stoughton, 2005), p143.

154 William Dodd, 'Thought on the Glorious Epiphany of Jesus Christ,' 1758.

155 JRR Tolkien in *The Messiah Comes to Middle-Earth*, ed. Philip Ryken (IVP, 2017), p23.

156 From a public letter written by Corrie Ten Boom in 1974 – here in full: www.tedmontgomery.com/bblovrvw/Rapture/corrie.html.

157 Stanley Grenz, *Theology for the Community of God* (Paternoster, 1994), p851.

158 CS Lewis, *Mere Christianity* (Harper Edition, 2001), p134.

159 Samuel Rutherford, *Letters of Samuel Rutherford* (Banner of Truth, 2006).

160 Joseph Esper, 'The Light of the World,' *Catholic Journal*, 28 September 2015, catholicjournal.us.